PRAISE
Air M

"With the element of air being vital to our everyday lives, it is not surprising that *Air Magic* is extensive and detailed. Astrea Taylor (and other voices in well-placed essays) offers accessible wisdom and personal knowing while sharing rituals that have helped me deepen my relationship with air. From the myths to the deities, to creatures and guardians (and a lot more!), this book offers the gift of expansiveness into what we cannot see, but we deeply know."

—Irisanya Moon, author of *Reclaiming Witchcraft* and *Aphrodite: Goddess of Love & Beauty & Initiation*

"*Air Magic* is a refreshing exploration of the element that is always with us. Perhaps using some air magic of her own to craft a book that is both clear and concise, Astrea leads the reader through history, personal experiences, and practices, providing an excellent overview for anyone interested in connecting with the power of this element."

—Cyndi Brannen, author of *Keeping Her Keys* and *Entering Hekate's Garden*

"*Air Magic* does a stellar job of breathing life into the magic of air. An element of creation and manifestation, travel and transformation, air is all around us and inside us. Astrea Taylor gives us everything we need to know about this vital element and much, much more."

—Lilith Dorsey, author of *Water Magic* and *Orishas, Goddesses, and Voodoo Queens*

AIR
MAGIC

© Elizabeth Krisher

Astrea Taylor is an eclectic/intuitive pagan Witch, writer, and speaker whose goals include empowering other Witches and encouraging them to use intuition in their witchcraft. She's the author of *Intuitive Witchcraft* (Llewellyn, 2020), and is well known for her blog *Starlight Witch* on Patheos Pagan. She has published passages in *The Witch's Altar, The Witches' Companion, Witchology Magazine, Soul & Spirit Magazine,* and *Lune Bleue Magazine.* When she's not co-leading the Aurora Fire dance group or writing rituals and astrology for the Blessed Be Box, she leads workshops and rituals at gatherings across the country. Learn more at www.AstreaTaylor.com.

Astrea Taylor

AIR MAGIC

Elements
of
Witchcraft

FIRST EDITION
Third Printing, 2023

Cover design by Shannon McKuhen

Llewellyn is a registered trademark of Llewellyn Worldwide Ltd.

Library of Congress Cataloging-In-Publication Data

Names: Taylor, Astrea, author.
Title: Air magic / Astrea Taylor.
Description: Woodbury, MN : Llewellyn Publications, a Division of Llewellyn Worldwide Ltd., 2021. | Series: Elements of witchcraft ; 2 | Includes bibliographical references and index.
Identifiers: LCCN 2020053380 (print) | LCCN 2020053381 (ebook) | ISBN 9780738764313 | ISBN 9780738764566 (ebook)
Subjects: LCSH: Witchcraft. | Magic. | Air—Miscellanea.
Classification: LCC BF1572.A37 T39 2021 (print) | LCC BF1572.A37 (ebook) | DDC 133.4/3—dc23
LC record available at https://lccn.loc.gov/2020053380
LC ebook record available at https://lccn.loc.gov/2020053381

Llewellyn Publications
A Division of Llewellyn Worldwide Ltd.
2143 Wooddale Drive
Woodbury, MN 55125-2989

www.llewellyn.com
Printed in the United States of America

For Tim,

whose love, wit, and creativity
inspire me every single day

CONTENTS

PART 2:
WORKING WITH THE ELEMENT OF AIR

PART 3:
RECIPES, RITUALS & SPELLCRAFT

The village Witch grew her own herbs, made her own charms, and perfected the art of the Witches' Craft through adherence to the ways handed down from generation to generation. The art of Witchcraft was also taught "on the voice of the wind," which reflects the teaching that spirits convey the old ways to those they deem worthy.

—*Raven Grimassi*

DISCLAIMER

The advice in this book is intended to educate and assist people on their quest to learn and become stronger practitioners of air magic. There are no absolute guarantees of outcomes, as much is outside of our control. Please ensure your personal safety at all times. For example, don't meditate and drive or operate heavy machinery at the same time. Be cautious when using oils and herbs—don't ingest essential oils, don't use undiluted essential oils on your skin, and be cautious in the use of herbs and essential oils in case an allergic reaction or a contraindication with medicine could occur. Consult a doctor, therapist, or another health care provider before ingesting any herbs or if you have any medical or mental health concerns.

Although this book contains information about several religions, cultural practices, deities, and more, it is not meant to be a complete resource or an instruction manual. If additional information is desired, it should be sought from a proper primary source.

FOREWORD

For centuries and through many esoteric practices, the elements have been the cornerstones of magical practice. Whether it's astrology or modern Witchcraft, these four basic elements create the boundaries and the structures within larger, multidimensional spiritual frameworks. They can bring concepts home and make them more readily understandable.

Earth is the ground we walk on, quite literally. It is the rocks, the mud, the mountains. Earth is also our body and the physical manifestation in this life. It is our center and our stability.

Fire is the flame in the hearth. It is the candle, the bonfire, the sun. Fire both warms and destroys. It has the power to transform and incite. Its flame is our passion and our will to go on.

Water is the rain from the skies. It is the world's oceans and lakes, the comforting bath, and the morning dew. Water is our blood and sweat, as well as our memories. It rules our emotions and manifests as tears.

Air is all around us. It is our breath, the sounds we hear, and the wind that touches our faces. Air carries seeds and pollen, scents that warn and delight, and songs of culture. Air is our voice, our thoughts, and our ideas.

While every esoteric system applies these basic concepts differently, the elements are there, helping to structure practice and develop a greater understanding of self. For modern Witches, the elements are often represented in their magical tools, where, for example, the cauldron might be water and the pentacle earth. For Wiccans more specifically, the elements help raise the magical circle and empower the protective quarters. In tarot, the elements flow through the symbolic imagery of the pip cards, and in astrology, the elements correspond to the signs, with three signs representing each element.

For still others, the elements simply provide spiritual guidance for daily meditations, visualizations, spell work, or life lessons. One might ask, what element do I need to get through today?

The following book is the second in a special series that dives deeply into the symbolism and magical use of the elements. Each book focuses on just one element, beginning with water. The books cover everything associated with the elements, from spiritual places and deities to practical spells and rituals. For the Witch who wants to envelop themselves in elemental practice or for someone who needs a resource on each the elements, this second book and its sisters will provide everything you need.

Written by four different authors from around the globe, the four books in the elemental magick series show just how wide and deep the esoteric understanding of the elements goes and how to make that concept work for your own magical and spiritual needs.

Join us on a deep exploration of, and journey through, the magical use of the four elements.

By Heather Greene
ACQUISITIONS EDITOR, LLEWELLYN WORLDWIDE

To Fly

Pixel Witch is a producer, drag queen, aerialist, and dancer. When she's not performing all around the world, she performs at The House of Yes in New York City.

Air magic is about transcendence.
What is more transcendent than a human off their feet?
Than flying?
To fly
is to transcend anything
anyone thought the human was capable of.
We do not have wings.
We do not jump very high.
We are ground animals.
And yet,
because of the curious minds of the artist,
the dreamer,
and the witch who thought
"what if?"
A human can fly.
To climb,
to get as far from the earth's mantle as possible,
is to fly—
is to perform magic.

Pixel Witch

• • • •

THE STIRRING WIND

Have you ever been outdoors on a stroll when a cool wind stirred up all the leaves around you? Perhaps the wind caressed your skin and played with your hair or clothing. You may have felt it move your spirit and promote a feeling of effervescence within you. You may have even felt that it's possible for you to take flight.

If you've ever dreamed about magical flight, you know that there's a certain familiarity to it. It's almost as if flying is a natural ability we have, and we merely have to remember how to fly. It can feel so powerful to fly in our dreams, far above the earth and free from our cares. It's a mystical, sublime feeling, and it's the perfect analogy for what the magical element of air feels like.

Since ancient times, people have studied the element of air. Over the millennia, they've concluded it's one of the four basic states of energy, along with earth, water, and fire. Air is associated with the mind, thinking, breath, inspiration, and imagination. It's also connected with communication, travel, change, elevation, spirits, and expansion. This book explores all of these airy qualities and reveals how modern Witches can use the power of air in their craft.

As someone who has studied air magic for several years, I felt called to write this book. I've studied several types of breath work, both in meditation and yoga. These practices revealed the direct connections between the spirit, the breath, and the mind. Likewise, from my college archery classes, I know that one's breath makes a huge difference when it comes to directing energy. A long, slow breath steadies the mind and lets the arrow hit the mark more often. As an environmental scientist, the scientific nature of air is in my wheelhouse. I've studied weather, storms, climate, and the ever-changing atmosphere. The creatures of air are familiar to me as well, and I've studied bats, birds, and butterflies. I also have direct experiences with spirits, astral projection, and weather witchery. On top of that, my natal astrological chart has several planets in all three air signs.

In my studies, I've formulated three different ways to relate to the element of air: the personal, the physical, and the magical. Each state embodies several distinctive qualities of air.

The Personal Element of Air: Breath, Mind, and Communication

Breathing gives us a very personal connection with the element of air. The constant flow of our lungs connects us with it at all times, vitally so. We breathe between seventeen thousand and twenty-three thousand times each day, which is more often than any other activity.[1] Take a brief moment to inhale deeply and connect with

---

1   Ann Brown, "How Many Breaths Do You Take Each Day?" The EPA Blog, published April 24, 2014, accessed July 3, 2019, https://blog.epa.gov/2014/04/28/how-many-breaths-do-you-take-each-day.

what's present in your lungs right now. If you even start to slow your breathing, there's a good chance you'll start to relax. On the other hand, if you start to breathe rapidly, you may become more alert and focused. Breath controls our mindsets, and it can be used to facilitate trance states and spiritual work.

Air is also associated with our minds. We use our brains every day, whether in the form of critical thinking, envisioning, organization, inventing, planning, learning, or any of the myriad other functions of the mind. An active mind is often linked to a whirlwind of ideas, brainstorms of creativity, and thunderbolts of inspiration.

Communication is another personal aspect of the element of air. Whenever we write, speak, or sing our words, we're expressing our thoughts. This act transforms them from our internal worlds and gives birth to them in the external world, creating new possibilities.

The Physical Element of Air: Expansion, Travel, and Change

Science reveals many of the secrets of the invisible world of air all around us, including the physical natures of air, which are expansion, travel, transportation, and change. Air is composed of several different gases, which have a natural preference to expand and travel as much as possible. Air molecules are constantly moving, usually at a much faster rate than solids or liquids. This movement and travel lets them come into contact with several different kinds of other molecules, and when the conditions are right, they change.

Air naturally transports all kinds of things. For example, the sound waves of a plucked harp string and the aroma of burning incense can easily travel through the air. Wind, or active air, even moves particles—this is evident in the way wind subtly carves away at mountains, blowing their dust on the wind to other locations. Wind also carries warmth, electricity, and humidity. When air fronts that are energetically different collide, they release this energy in the form of lightning, thunder, and rain.

Air is constantly changing. The different elements and molecules of air are constantly being released, fixed, or changed into something else. The air you're breathing at this very moment may have once been part of an aloe plant, a coral reef, a scarlet macaw, a drop in Lake Victoria, or a tar pit.

The Magical Element of Air:
Creation, Manifestation, Spirits, and Deities

The magical element of air surrounds us at all times. We're immersed in it. You could think of it as an invisible world filled with energy, spirits, and deities. You could also think of it as its own energetic plane or realm. Our thoughts and words are in constant communication with this realm. The magical element of air receives our thoughts, brainwaves, and psychic communications—it translates them into energy and transmits them out into the world. This is how manifestation magic works.

Whenever we enter a trance state, our minds and spirits shift into the frequency of the magical element of air, which allows us to communicate with the spirits and deities who reside there. The magical realm of air is also where our spirits travel when we astrally project.

Bringing the Air Aspects Together

We often experience all three aspects of the element of air at the same time. This is how a spirit can reside within a body. This is also how plants and rocks have air energy. The magical realm of air connects the physical plane with the higher spiritual planes. It's all connected—the rate of our breathing changes our mindset, which creates our thoughts, which help us choose words. When these words are expressed, they transmit energy back out into the magical realm of air, where it travels far and wide, and eventually attracts the same energy back to us.

Air energy has a natural flow, with energy coming in and going out constantly. This could be seen as energy being received and transmitted, whether through the breath, the mind, communication and listening, or the spirit giving and receiving energy.

When working with the element of air, use whichever aspects and characteristics of air inspire you to truly feel the element on all three levels. Feel the air all around you, your thoughts, and the spirits that reside therein. Use your breath, senses, and spirit! Call upon whatever moves the element of air within you and inspires you to feel light as a feather.

Up, Up, and Away!

When you're ready to rise up into the magical element of air and learn more, take a deep breath. Consider the fresh start and all the information and wisdom you could glean. Envision all of your intentions becoming true in detail. When you're ready, activate the air energy of new beginnings, and turn the page.

PART
1

HISTORY,
FOLKLORE & MYTH

Up the airy mountain,
Down the rushy glen,
We daren't go a-hunting
For fear of little men.

—WILLIAM ALLINGHAM, "THE FAIRIES"

Chapter 1

AIR THROUGHOUT TIME AND CULTURE

Air, thought, and breath are powerful concepts that are all tied to the spirit. There's evidence of this in archaeology, etymology, art, worship, and mythology. Several themes of the element of air are prevalent throughout history, but perhaps the most telling of all of these is the development of the human mind and spirit over time. Human minds were shaped by the advent of thought, which eventually brought about knowledge, and sometimes wisdom. The path of the human spirit parallels not only that of the mind but also how other spirits were viewed.

Let's fly back in time to view human history through the scope of the element of air through the mind and spirit. Through its developments, challenges, and triumphs, the power of air comes through. Although this chapter doesn't cover a complete history of the mind and spirit (and likely no one chapter ever could), the most prominent Western trends are included, as well as some world history.

Chapter 1

Prehistoric Mentality: Animism

At the dawn of human consciousness in the Stone Age, an animist mindset likely prevailed. The word animism comes from the Latin word *animas*, which translates to the philosophy of the breath, mind, and soul. This is the belief and inner knowing that everything is alive, with a spirit and its own intelligence. It's a very connected way of looking at the world. Because this magical mindset likely occurred for several thousands of years, it's thought to have set the tone for the subconscious.

The Neolithic era marked a change when thought became more prevalent. In this brave new era, people began to conceive of a future, and they started planning for it. This time saw the emergence of innovations such as agriculture, domestication of animals, and the construction of permanent homes. Inventions arose to solve common problems, and this era had a more developed spiritual aspect as well. The animistic mindset was slightly modified as people saw the natural world as yet another problem they could solve with their minds. Deities were born—instead of seeing wind as a mysterious living force, it became a specific spirit or deity with a name and a story. It could be engaged with through offerings, reverence, and dialogue. Much of animism remained, but these deities were seen as more powerful than the animistic spirits—more as a ruling or royal class of spirits as opposed to nature spirits. Religions arose during this era, and the ancient pagan religions were created.

Permanent dwellings and villages created communities of people who found it beneficial to come together during certain times. They created rituals to celebrate the new gods and to mark the seasons. This era also saw the veneration of the deceased through burial sites and funerary rituals. Stone monuments were erected in this time, including Stonehenge and the Great Pyramids. There was also a huge increase in communication, art, and refining of language.

Ancient History: Magic

The pre-historic era ended when history began to be recorded, that is, with the invention of the written word. Pagan rituals and myths were documented in works such as *The Iliad* and *The Odyssey*. They provide a glorious snapshot of ancient beliefs. With more sophisticated methods of communication and reason, this era fostered the births of poetry, magic, science, philosophy, more developed religion, refined art, astronomy, math, and much more. These areas of study were all considered ways to understand and influence the universe, and they were not separated.

Despite the vast distances between most ancient cultures, several air-related themes emerged, including air's powers of creation, the philosophy of air as a magical element, the belief that air is connected with spirits, and more. Here are a few of the ancient air themes.

Air Creation Stories

Countless stories of the creation of the universe, earth, life, and humanity start with the element of air. This could be a breath, a spoken word, or a deity associated with air. All of these tie into air's association with beginnings and initiations.

Air is predominant in the Greek origin myths. They believed that the universe was created when a shapeless being called Chaos gave birth to Night, a goddess with dark wings. Night laid an egg from which the entire universe was born. The earth was created with the merging of the god who embodied the sky and air, Ouranos, and Gaia, the earth goddess. Humanity was created by Prometheus and Epimetheus, gods whose names mean forethought and afterthought.

The North Indian Minyong tribespeople also believed in a creator sky god and a creatress earth goddess. These deities gave birth to the first people.

The ancient Chinese believed the universe was the shape of an egg, sometimes called the cosmic egg. From it came air or breath (known as *Qi*, *Chi*, or *Ki*). This air also created the earth and all life, including humanity.

Tahitian myths involve a cosmic egg, from which emerged a god who created the universe and humans.

The Huron Nation of Native Americans believed the first human, a woman, fell from a tear in the sky.

In ancient Egypt, Thoth, the god of wisdom, writing, and magic, spoke words to create himself. He then laid the egg that became the world. Ra is also credited with creating the heavens, earth, and people. A mythological bird called the benu was born at the same time as the world, and every morning at sunrise, it's reborn along with the rising sun.

In Mayan myths, a feathered serpent and a deity known as the Heart of the Sky created the physical world with their words and thoughts. They went on to form humans, language, writing, and books, too.

The Yoruba people of Nigeria believed a spirit named Olorun was the ruler of the sky. He ordered the creation of the earth and gave life to humanity.

Other ancient religions including Judaism and Christianity believed that a spoken word birthed the cosmos and the earth. This kind of thinking is evident in our modern language—even the word universe translates to "one song."

Philosophy of Air as a Magical Element

Several ancient civilizations believed in basic elements, or energies of which everything else was composed. This notion originated from all over the world, including the ancient civilizations in Greece, Japan, China, parts of Africa, India, Tibet, Hawaii, and Northern Europe. The numbers of these elements ranged from three to seven. Empedocles, a Greek philosopher and magician of the fifth century BCE, thought of the elements as spiritual essences, which each had their own powerful god-like energy. These sentiments are echoed by Anaximenes, a Greek philosopher from about 500 BCE, who believed that air created the universe and the world, and it was the source of all of the other elements.

The philosophy of the element of air was developed in this era. Aristotle declared that the nature of air was warm and moist. In the fourth century BCE, the Greek physician Hippocrates associated air with blood because it was hot and moist. Around 300 BCE, the alchemist Zosimos was the first to associate air with a cardinal direction: south. Hermes Trismegistus, an Egyptian sage circa 200 CE, furthered the concepts of air elemental correspondences.

Breath Contains Spirit and Life

The association between breath and spirit makes sense—breathing is the first sign of life after birth, and it's one of the last things we do before we pass from this world. As such, breath (or air) is thought by many cultures to be life or spirit itself. In Greek and

Latin, the word *psyche* translates to breath, vitality, life, and spirit. The root word of breathe, from the Latin *spirair*, is associated with the words spirit, inspiration, and aspiration. *Pneumea* is the Greek word for breath and spirit. The Hebrew word *ruach* translates to breath, air, wind, and spirit.

Some deities, such as Yahweh, Odin, and Olorun, breathed life into the first people. The Navajo tribespeople believe that the first breath of a baby determines their fate. In some Native American practices, a shaman can capture a fragmented piece of a soul in their lungs and blow it back into a person—the shaman's breath has the power to reunite the broken shards of a soul. Another connection between breath and spirit is that breath is thought by many people to be the key to clearing the mind and achieving astral projection.

The Air Contains Spirits or Deities

Many ancient civilizations believed that spirits lived in the air. In ancient Greece, these were called *daimons*, and they were thought of as a beneficial or harmless group of spirits that included nature spirits, the souls of the dead, guardians, and tutelary guides.[2] Daimons could act on the behalf of humans in the world, and they were also intermediaries between humans and the gods.

In some ancient cultures, winds were associated with spirits. The Irish legend of the sidhe, or the spirits known as the Fae, literally translates to "gust of wind" or "folk of the air."[3] Similarly,

---

2   "Daimon," Online Etymology Dictionary, accessed December 28, 2019, https://www.etymonline.com/word/daimon.

3   Ottis Bedney Sperlin, *Studies in English-World Literature*, (New York: Century Company, 1923), 268.

strong winds were characterized as horses made of air in some cultures. The "Wild Hunt" is a European myth about a collection of spirits, led by Odin, who ride ghostly horses, make the winds howl, and portend doom to those who see them.

In many cultures, the wind was personified as a deity. In the Navajo Native American religion, the Holy Wind is the omniscient, all-powerful entity that makes everything happen. They believe everything has this internal wind, which could be translated to spirit. Some cultures, including the Egyptians, Greeks, Romans, Celts, Native Americans, and the Norse, had a deity for each of the "four winds," or the winds from four cardinal directions. These deities were each associated with an energy, a temperature, and a season.

The Mind Is an Energy Center

Another common theme that arose from this time is that the mind contains a nexus of energy related to thinking, visualizing, communicating, and other airy aspects. This is clear in the Hindu sixth chakra, the Norse *hugr*, the Sufi *nafs*, the Celtic *Coire Sois* (viewed as a cauldron), and the Huna *uhane*, which is called both the conscious mind and the spirit.

Middle Ages: Repression of the Mind and Spirit

The Middle Ages began just after the fall of Rome in 476 CE. Pagan religions waned as patriarchal religions rose in prominence in the Western world. Some historians believe this change was congruous with a mental shift that occurred due to the invention of linear writing. By 538 CE, the Roman Church had banned all pagan worship. The few pagan practices that were not obliterated were stripped of their original meanings and incorporated into Church practices. Scientific, alchemical, and magical studies were forbidden. Several alchemists fled to parts of the Middle East, where there was greater religious tolerance.

For much of the Western world, it was an unenlightened age. Few people could read, and books were kept in private libraries due to their great cost. However, despite the growing power of the Church, some paganism and folklore survived. In the eighth and ninth centuries, several Church officials recorded testimonies of women who reported that they flew, apparently by astral projection or dreams, in the night skies with other people, animals, the goddess Diana, and/or supernatural beings. The tale of the Witch flying through the night sky may have arisen from these descriptions.

In the eleventh and twelfth centuries, newly translated books arrived in Europe from Arabic, Jewish, and Greek sources, which sparked a renewed interest in learning. People learned about philosophy, astronomy, astrology, science, alchemy, magic, spirit communication, divination, and topics such as the magical powers of stones and plants. The abundance of information provided a foundation for medieval magic and what is known as the "twelfth-century renaissance."

At this time, Church officials likely read the ancient texts about daimons and interpreted them as evil spirits. This is presumed from the invention of the word *demon* around 1200, meaning, "an evil spirit ... a devil."[4] The Church considered all spirits evil, includ-

---

4   "Demon," Online Etymology Dictionary, accessed December 28, 2019, https://www.etymonline.com/word/demon.

ing the old gods, the dead, nature spirits, the spirits of place, and folkloric spirits like faeries, elves, and brownies. These "demons" were associated with the element of air and with the "devil," who was called, "the Prince of the Power of the Air."[5]

The literal demonization of the very air that was necessary for breathing created a fearful perspective of life as a constant battle between good and evil. The Church grew increasingly paranoid of people invoking and communicating with these spirits, in what they called necromancy. In 1239, the Church formed the Inquisition, whose goal was to eliminate heresy and evil as well as rebels. An estimated forty thousand to sixty thousand people were killed, and many more were tortured in a bloodbath that continued for several centuries into the Enlightenment. Nonetheless, new magical books were still published and circulated, even under the possible punishment of death.

Renaissance: A Cautious Rebirth

Renaissance means rebirth, and it's a suitable name for an era when the invention of the printing press allowed topics such as the classical arts, sciences, and philosophy to flourish once again. Books and pamphlets were copied quickly, and information was spread on a wide scale, which encouraged literacy and mental development. However, not all of the information printed in this era was beneficial. In 1487, the Inquisition produced the *Malleus Maleficarum,* a Witch hunter's guide for detecting, torturing, and killing Witches.

Despite the severity of the inquisitions, the occult sciences secretly bloomed with the help of printing presses. The word

5   Eph 2:2 KJV.

"occult" was invented around 1520; it means "to cover up or conceal."[6] It was necessary to hide arcane knowledge from those who would destroy it. Magical orders were founded, and they circulated pamphlets. During this era, several books were published that hypothesized about the nature of air.

The Renaissance ended in the mid-1600s when the philosopher Descartes developed new reductionist philosophies that prioritized rational thinking. Logic and reason began to infiltrate common thought, and it sowed the seeds for the Age of Enlightenment. In a backlash and an attempt to repress freedom of thought and spirit, Witch hunts escalated.

The Age of Enlightenment: Greater Freedom of Thought and Spirit

The Age of Enlightenment, starting around 1715, marked a time when people were generally more educated than ever before in the past thousand years. They questioned authority, valued reason, and revered freedom of expression. All of these airy principles started to loosen the stranglehold of religion and fearful superstition.

With greater freedom of thought, several new occult books were copied and published that contributed to more material than ever before. More secret societies formed, such as the Freemasons and the Hellfire Club. Although the Inquisition raged on in countries like France, Germany, Switzerland, and Poland, this era eventually marked the last person to be executed for witchcraft in Europe or North America, in 1793.

6   "Occult," Dictionary, accessed December 28, 2019, https://www.dictionary.com/browse/occult.

In the late 1700s, the Romantic era arose, with greater freedom of expression in art. A love of the macabre and the mysterious took off in literature by writers such as Keats and Shelley, who often used pagan deities in their works. New art and spiritual movements began. This era also was when Haitian practitioners of Vodoun emigrated to New Orleans, which helped establish the religion of Voodoo. A Druidic revival movement also started in this era when Druids held a ceremony honoring the autumn equinox in 1798.

In the 1800s, the Romantic era continued to flourish in the middle of the Industrial Revolution. Several new occult and mystical books were published, and many older ones were republished. *The Magus*, published in 1801, influenced ceremonial magicians for centuries to come. In 1820, the *Long Lost Friend* was published. This book of recipes and spells with a Christian slant became associated with the rebirth of folk magic and a practice known as Hoodoo.

Spiritualism: Revived Spirits

The Spiritualist movement began in 1848 with an interest in seances and mediumship, which soon became widespread across Europe and North America. This curiosity also provoked studies of the occult, ancient paganism, and spiritual practices in other parts of the world.

During this era, Éliphas Lévi, a Hermetic alchemist and ceremonial magician, published several occult books. He appeared to have a great affinity with the element of air, as he revered knowledge above all. He developed the elemental axioms, including *to know* for air, and named the elemental rulers of air the

Paralda. He furthered the understanding of correspondences and ritualized magic.

Many spiritual advances occurred in the latter part of this century. From 1850 to 1869, Marie Laveau became the renowned leader of the New Orleans Voodoo community. Helena Blavatsky promoted occult philosophies. This era inspired the creation of the word *neopagan* around 1875[7] and the formation of several groups and esoteric societies. These included Norse pagan groups and the *Societas Rosicruciana in Anglia*, which led to the Hermetic Order of the Golden Dawn, who coined the phrase "watchtowers of the east" to summon the elemental rulers of the air. Aleister Crowley, a member of several esoteric groups including the Hermetic Order of the Golden Dawn, further popularized ceremonial magic. Other authors of the era, including Charles Leland and Margaret Murray, published books with premises that unbroken witchcraft religions continued from the Roman Empire. Although many of their ideas were unfounded, they reflected a common idealization of magic, myth, and resistance in that era.

Rebirth of Witchcraft: The Secret is Out

In 1951, the British anti-witchcraft act was repealed. The same year, Robert Cochrane started Traditional Witchcraft, a non-pagan witchcraft movement. In 1954, Gerald Gardner published *Witchcraft Today*, in which he revealed the practice of Wicca, a previously unknown version of witchcraft.

In the 1960s, the counterculture was born. Many people parted with social conformity and organized religions, and there was a

7 "Neopaganism," ibid, accessed December 21, 2019, https://www.dictionary.com/browse/neopaganism.

push toward greater equality. The New Age movement arose from the ashes of spiritualism during this time. This newer way of thinking incorporated the power of positive thought and a search for spiritual meaning outside the social norms. People began exploring ways to connect the mind, body, and spirit, which was reflected in the increasing popularity of Eastern practices such as meditation and yoga. Many were drawn toward nature, paganism, and witchcraft.

Several books about witchcraft were published, some of which advocated for a solitary study, self-initiation, and a more intuitive approach to magic and witchcraft.

Globalization: The Age of Information

The internet changed everything—information was shared more widely and easily than ever before, and people connected across the world, even if it wasn't in "real life." Social media also connected people with knowledge from all over the world. Many people call this era the Age of Information and the Age of Aquarius. This is fitting, considering the element of air is more prevalent now than ever before in humanity's era. Information is literally in the air in the form of wifi and cellular connections. Other popular air technologies include microwaves, wind power, drones, and LiDAR. And of course, you've probably heard the term for data banks—the cloud. This era is such a perfect embodiment of the element of air that we might as well call it the "Age of Air."

For many people, this unparalleled freedom and information coincides with a feeling of disillusionment with the current establishments. The solution? Witchcraft. More people are studying witchcraft than ever before. From 2008 to 2018, the Witch, pagan, and occult population is estimated to have doubled in the United States to a total of 1.5 million practitioners.[8] Books about witchcraft, paganism, and the occult are being published and sold at greater rates than ever before, and the "trend" doesn't appear to be slowing down.[9] Practitioners of the magical arts view them as spiritual practices and ways to exercise more power in their lives.

The Age of Information also has a unique crisis that's intimately connected with the element of air. The accumulation of greenhouse gases in the earth's atmosphere has been creating changes in climate that may be irreversible.

Fortunately, we can use the element of air to help solve the dilemmas of our era. We can use discernment when it comes to information and the choices available to us. We can exercise wisdom in our consumerism, and we can communicate with our officials to pass laws that mitigate climate change. Hopefully, with new inventions and innovations, we will continue to thrive in this age and achieve mental and spiritual freedom for everyone on the planet.

8   Melissa Malamut, "Witch Population Doubles as Millennials Cast Off Christianity," *New York Post*, published November 20, 2018, accessed December 28, 2019. https://nypost.com/2018/11/20/witch-population-doubles-as-millennials-cast-off-christianity/.

9   Lynn Garrett, "Season of the Witch: Mind Body Spirit Books," *Publishers Weekly*, published August 2, 2019, accessed December 28, 2019. https://www.publishersweekly.com/pw/by-topic/new-titles/adult-announcements/article/80847-season-of-the-witch-mind-body-spirit-books.html.

Conclusion

The element of air, in the form of the human mind and spirit, has grown alongside humanity. History may not always be pretty, but it's important to know where we came from. If history does repeat itself, we're forearmed with foreknowledge. With the spread of free thought and the ability to choose our own spiritual paths, the mind and spirit have soared to brave new heights. The future is unwritten, but it's likely that the thirst for knowledge, freedom, and equality will continue to grow to unparalleled dimensions.

Chapter 2

MYTHOLOGICAL AIR BEASTS AND PLACES

Many mythical beings and locations are associated with the magic of air. Creatures such as dragons, gryphons, and faeries are a part of the collective human consciousness and imagination. They can be found in nearly every art form since the beginning of recorded time: in paintings, woodcuts, pottery, frescoes, myths, stories, and on coats of arms. These airy mythological beings are featured in stories that thrilled and terrified ancient audiences. Likewise, mythological locations of air are found in nearly every culture, and they inspired wonder and longing for these other worlds.

For millennia, many of these myths were thought to actually exist. The common belief in these creatures and locations was due to first-hand accounts of experiences, and to books that included both imaginary and real creatures. It was thought that perhaps only a few people had experienced these myths because the creatures were rare, or the way to the mythical location was inaccessible, or the beings of these otherworlds kidnapped anyone who drew near and returned them decades or centuries later.

When logic started to overrule superstition in the seventeenth and eighteenth centuries, views of these myths changed. Adults were expected to be rational and not entertain illogical or fantastical notions. With the continued lack of proof of existence, mythological beasts were finally categorized as fantastical creatures. Likewise, faery tales that were once enjoyed by all ages were relegated to children only.

However, the myths lived on in the form of fairy tales, fables, bestiary books, and legends like those told by the Grimm Brothers, Andrew Lang, and J. R. R. Tolkien. These days, airy beings and locations are entrenched in modern art, movies, television shows, and books. It's nearly impossible to imagine *Game of Thrones* without flying dragons, or Fillory, the imaginary realm of *The Magicians*, without faeries.

Think of the myths in this chapter as whimsical views, archetypes, and personifications of the magical element of air. Let them inspire you to feel more in touch with the element of air by lifting your imagination. I encourage you to dance with sylphs in spirals of incense smoke. Imagine a majestic gryphon flying overhead and feel your heart soar. Search the clouds for those castles made of air. Let these stories elevate your mind and spirit, as they were intended to do.

Mythical Creatures of Air

Winged and Flying Dragons

Dragons were once thought to be the largest creatures on earth. They flew through the air with ease and caused all kinds of weather, especially thunderstorms. Good dragons healed and helped people, but evil dragons consumed livestock and people, and they burned entire villages with one pass of their fiery breath. In medieval England, there were eyewitness accounts of massive, scaly dragons that flew on bat-like wings and terrorized towns. The legendary King Arthur was associated with dragons so much so that he wore an emblem of one on his helmet. Some historians believed that dragons were a symbol of the ancient pagan culture and a symbol of resistance against Christianity. Conquering an evil dragon was often a euphemism for overcoming an inner struggle to achieve the liberation of the soul from mental and emotional constraints.

In ancient China, dragons were powerful masters of the element of air and bearers of good fortune. They play in the clouds, rolling around and sometimes chasing a sphere of light. These dragons can become as big as the entire sky or as small as a tiny worm. As lords of the weather, they direct the wind, clouds, and rain. Although the dragons have the ability to cause storms, they only damage people's property if the dragons aren't happy with their behavior.

Magically, dragons are associated with ambition, the subconscious, challenges, protection and destruction, dreams, weather, enlightenment, ancient wisdom, luck, fertility, balance, manifestation, the otherworlds, power, courage, wealth, creativity, and protection. These magnificent creatures may also be associated with other elements, depending on their anatomy, abilities, and habitat. Similar to the dragon are the mythological creatures the wyvern (a dragon with a fish tail) and the cockatrice (a dragon with a fish tail and a rooster's head).

Winged Serpents

Winged serpents are found in folklore all over the world, including ancient Europe, India, China, Japan, Central and North America, Hawaii, New Zealand, Finland, Egypt, and the Middle East. They're the same size as regular serpents, only they have beautiful, feathered wings.

Legends vary about the inclinations of winged serpents. In some tales, they're protectors and guardians that act on behalf of the good of humanity. The Phoenicians called them *agathosdaimon,* which translates to a protector spirit. In a Chinese tale, winged serpents arrive at a home and warn the family about a coming drought. However, other tales say that winged serpents are dangerous and antagonistic. Their bites caused disease and their urine dissolved flesh. Arabian winged snakes called *syrens* had venom that killed instantly, and they could even outrun a horse.

Several Egyptian deities were depicted as winged serpents, including the goddesses Mertseger, guarder of tombs; and Nekhebet, presider over childbirth and motherhood. The goddess Buto, the pharaoh's guardian, was also shown as a winged serpent, and is sometimes depicted wearing a crown as well.

In ancient Mayan tribal cultures, the feathered serpent Kukulcan was worshipped as a benevolent transformative deity. Centuries later, the legend of Kukulcan became Quetzalcoatl, an Aztec god depicted as a feathered serpent.

The Native American Cheyenne tribespeople have a cautionary legend of a winged serpent. One day, when two men were hunting, they came across a giant nest with the biggest eggs they'd ever seen. One man was hungry and ate an entire egg. Several days later, he started transforming into a giant feathered serpent. He grew feathers and scales all over his body. He was so miserable that he threw himself into a river. According to at least one account, this is the reason why the Cheyenne tribespeople always leave an offering of tobacco or food whenever they cross a river or a lake.

Bird Dragons

The Illini Native American tribe has the legend of the giant *piasa*, also known as the bird dragon, or the bird that devours men. This creature has an eighteen-foot wingspan, scales, antlers, bat wings, a long scaly tail, and the face of an angry man. It was originally a benevolent beast, but after assisting the Illini in battle, it developed a taste for human flesh. When it absconded with several members of the Illini tribe, it had to be killed. Its likeness can be found on cliff faces in the area to this day.

In Japanese myths, bird dragons were considered the most advanced form of all dragons. They were described as having a bird's body, a dragon's head, a beard, and a long mustache that trailed behind them as they flew.

Fire Birds

Several mythological birds are associated with the elements of air and fire. The most widely known of these is the phoenix, a multicolored eagle-sized bird native to Arabian regions that has a lifespan of several hundred years. When it's time for the phoenix to die, it creates a nest of spices, frankincense, and myrrh. It then flies toward the sun, catches fire, falls into the nest, and dies. After a few days, it rises from the ashes, reborn. The phoenix is associated with alchemy, turning lead into gold, and refining the soul. This magical bird is also associated with beauty, spirituality, new beginnings, happiness, strength, hope, destruction, longevity, the otherworlds, and rebirth and renewal.

The origin of the phoenix is thought to be the Egyptian *benu*, a mythological bird shaped like a heron that was born during the creation of the world. Every morning at sunrise, the benu is reborn along with the sun. It's connected with the worship of the sun gods Ra and Atum, and it accompanies the souls of the dead through the underworld. Hieroglyphics depicting the benu are often found carved onto the gold-plated tops of pyramids.

The *feng huang* is a beautiful Chinese fire bird that was born from the sun. It has multicolored plumage, a long reddish-gold tail, and both male and female qualities. This mythological bird represents half of royal matrimony; the royal dragon being the other half. It sings sweet songs and is credited with giving the musical scales to humanity. The feng huang appears as an omen during a peaceful time, or when a powerful leader is about to be born.

The Russian legend of the fire bird is of a bird whose feathers are actually on fire. Through mystical powers, the bird is not harmed. Similarly, the *caristae* is a bird that can fly through fire without harm. The *aitvaras* is a legendary Lithuanian rooster with a tail made of fire and dragon legs; it exchanges fortune, wealth, and plentiful grains for a homemade omelet.

Great Birds

Giant birds are legendary across the world. One of the most well-known great birds is the roc, a bird that was feared from Sumeria to China. Its name is derived from the Arabian word *ruach*, meaning breath of life. Some believe the roc is a giant raven, and others say it's an eagle, vulture, or condor. It's so strong that it flies away with people and even elephants to feed to its chicks. Some say that rocs live at the north star and that one of them laid an egg that became the world. The most famous account of a roc is in *The Arabian Nights*. When Sinbad is stranded in the ocean, a roc rescues him. Similar to the roc is the *anka*, a huge Arabian bird with a wingspan of over fifty feet.

The thunderbird legend comes from several Native American tribes across North America. This gigantic bird creates a clap of thunder every time it flaps its wings. It's so big that when it flies, water falls from the lake that exists on its back, and it makes rain fall in giant puddles. When the thunderbird is near the ocean, it hunts whales. And when it's inland, it battles the horned water snakes that live in the bottom of ponds and lakes. Magically, it's associated with intelligence, power, strength, and magic.

Another great bird was the *stymphalid*, a giant crane of Greek mythological origin, whose beak, feathers, and talons were made of the sharpest brass. *Stymphalids* could shoot their feathers, which sailed through the air like deadly knives and could easily pierce through even the thickest armor. They were known for consuming people whole and wiping out several villages. After Hercules killed most of them, they flew away to the far corners of the world, never to be seen again.

The Maori people of New Zealand have a legend of a giant eagle that is so big it can pick up children and fly away with them. Similarly, the *halulu* is a giant bird from Hawaii who also hunts people.

The Celestial Rooster, or the Bird of Dawn, is an enormous rooster from China whose cries at sunrise shake the whole world awake. Legend has it that all of the other roosters in the world originated from him. Another notable great bird reference is the giant chicken legs that carry around Baba Yaga's hut through the dark forests.

Magical Birds

Some birds might seem to be normal, but upon closer examination, you'd find they're actually magical. One example is the Persian *caladrius*, a white bird that has the ability to heal people. As long as someone is not mortally sick, the caladrius takes on their illness. This makes its feathers turn gray. It then flies toward the sun and disperses the sickness into the air. Its feathers turn white again, and once it returns to earth, it can heal again. The *hōm* is another bird that heals pain and wounds. It's associated with purity and divinity, and it also acts as a messenger.

Odin has two magical ravens: *Hugin*, meaning thought; and *Munin*, meaning memory. The wise birds tell him of all the things that happen across the world so that his wisdom will never truly end.

An Iranian magical bird known as the *huma* is a pure spirit that embodies both male and female qualities together. It's rarely seen, but when someone does catch a glimpse of it, it's said they'll be happy for the rest of their lives. When it flies directly over a person, that person will become a ruler. It's sometimes called the bird of fortune or the bird of paradise.

The *cucuio* is a legendary West Indies bird about the size of a thumb that creates its own light through its eyes. They're often caught and caged so they can light up the night with their eerie glowing eyes. This bird is thought to be related to the mythological German *ercinee*, a bird with phosphorescent feathers; and also the *alicanto*, a Chilean bird who glows after eating gold or silver.

Another magical bird is the two- or three-headed eagle. With their eyes seeing far in multiple locations, these birds saw all and knew all. They were widespread symbols of power in Roman and Celtic lore, and their majestic images survive on flags and coats of arms.

In Mexican folklore, some Witches can magically transform themselves into *la lechusa*, an owl who torments the wicked and foretells a death.

Human Hybrids

Human-animal hybrid creatures were very popular in mythology because it showed both the animalistic side of humans and the human side of animals. One of the most famous human hybrids is the siren—a nightingale with the head, and sometimes chest, of beautiful people, usually women. In ancient Greek legends, sirens mesmerized sailors with their enchanting songs. Once the men were enchanted, they steered their boats toward the sirens' island, where the sirens tore them apart and consumed their flesh. One legend said they were originally the handmaidens of Persephone. When she went missing, Demeter changed them into half-birds so they could fly far and wide and search for her. Stories of the Greek sirens likely inspired the Russian *sirin*, a giant owl with a woman's head and chest who sings lovely songs; and the Slavic *gamayun* and *alkonost*, both of whom enchanted people with their songs.

Harpies are a similar Greek mythological hybrid to the siren; however, these fearsome creatures had the bodies of vultures and the faces of angry old women. They're described as the spirits of abrupt, sharp winds. As the hounds of Zeus, harpies often absconded with unlawful people to deliver them to the Furies, the goddesses of vengeance.

The *conchon* is an eerie South American creature with a woman's head, a bird's body, and ears so large that it uses them to fly. This frightening sight warns people of bad luck.

The Japanese *tengu* are men who have beaks and wings. They cause mischief and harm wherever they go.

The Persian *simurgh* is a brilliant copper peacock with lion claws and a woman's head. Its name translates to "moon bird." Although it's large enough to carry off people and animals, it's a benevolent and all-knowing creature. Its very presence purifies the land. As one of the only birds with the ability to reason and communicate, it carries messages between the earth and the sky. In the famous story *The Conference of the Birds*, all of the birds search for it, which they call the greatest of all birds.

The Greek winged sphinx is a cunning beast with a human head, the body of a lion, and eagle wings. Sphinxes enacted justice by devouring people who were cruel and assisting those who were good. They also played riddles and mind games with people. If a sphinx didn't receive the right answer from someone, they often consumed the person. Magically, sphinxes are associated with the Greek goddess Athena, death, destruction, and magic.

Similar to the sphinx is the *buraq*, with the head of a man, the ears of a donkey, the body of a horse, and the feathers of a peacock. This creature is associated with purity, and it elevates people to the highest heavenly realms possible.

We could mention the depiction of fairies as tiny winged humans in this section; however, the historical version of fairies were not depicted that way. This more modern depiction stems from the romantic notions of the Victorian era and it may actually be more comparable to a sylph, an air elemental spirit.

Flying Animal Hybrids

The invention of mismatched mythological animals might have been a way to turn familiar beasts into conglomerate monsters. By giving them all of the scariest body parts, it likely ensured terror and very dramatic storytelling entertainment.

Gryphons are known as the King of the Beasts and were thought to be the largest birds in existence. They have the heads, wings, forearms, and talons of a giant eagle, and the body, legs, and tail of a lion. Gryphons are often seen in art from ancient Egypt, Ethiopia, Persia, and Greece, as well as art from the Renaissance. They're usually depicted as protectors, but they're also known to capture people or horses and feed them to their young. Gryphons are so strong that they could make off with a full-grown elephant or buffalo. They guard their treasures of gems and precious metals with their lives. In Greek mythology, gryphons are called the hounds of Zeus, and they are also associated with Athena and Apollo. They're connected with deities from Crete, Mesopotamia, and Egypt as well. Magically, gryphons are associated with strength and the connection between life and death. In Dante Alighieri's *Divine Comedy*, a gryphon leads a procession toward paradise.

Garudas, also known as Indian gryphons, are the size of wolves, and they have black feathers and a vibrant, red plumed chest. Similarly, the hippogriff is a gryphon with a horse's torso and rear legs. This creature first came about in the Renaissance and was inspired by Virgil's *Eclogues*. Perhaps the most famous literary hippogriff is Buckbeak in the Harry Potter series, who valiantly fights against the forces of evil.

Pegasi are magnificent winged horses from Greek mythology. They're the personification of a particularly swift wind and are associated with Zeus and storms. Pegasus, the first winged horse, was thought to have sprung from the blood of Medusa. Bellerophon, a Greek mortal, was able to tame Pegasus when he was given a golden bridle from the goddess Athena. However, in a similar story to that of Icarus and the wax wings, when Bellerophon tried to fly on Pegasus to Mount Olympus to become a god, Pegasus cast him off his back to fall to his death. Pegasus dwells in a stable on Mount Olympus amongst the other horses of Zeus. He is permitted to bring thunder and lightning whenever Zeus wishes. Pegasi with horns were native to Ethiopia.

Perytons are creatures with the front half of a buck, and the wings, rear legs, and tail of a great bird. They're the mortal enemy of people and will fight them to the death without hesitation. Originally from Atlantis, they survived the destroying earthquake by flying into the air.

And of course, who could forget the flying monkeys in *The Wizard of Oz*? Although they did the bidding of a wicked Witch who could also fly, they had a gray morality. When they were free from the Witch of the West, they didn't impede the protagonists any longer. Other flying animal hybrids include winged bulls, seen in Persian art dating back to at least the eighth century BCE, and lions with wings, which are often found in medieval art.

Wingless Flying Animals

Norse myths are rich with animals that can fly even though they have no wings. The giants known as Day and Night ride wingless horse-drawn chariots across the sky and are chased by flying wolves. The Norse god Odin rides a wingless eight-legged horse named Sleipnir who flies through the sky and travels into the underworld. He rides this horse while leading the Wild Hunt, the ghastly brigade of spirits who ride horses and other beasts as they fly through the air in pursuit of their prey. In the Norse *Prose Edda*, a wingless flying horse called Hófvarpnir is mentioned briefly. Even Thor's sky chariot is pulled by a pair of wingless goats.

The first recorded myth of the wingless flying reindeer goes back to Christmas poems from the 1820s. Since then, the legend of reindeer who fly with magical powers has become widespread, especially during the winter holiday season.

Mythical Beings

Sylphs

Just as there are nymph spirits that reside in forests, streams, the ocean, volcanoes, and other natural places, there are spirits of the element of air, which are sometimes called sylphs. These elementals or air spirits are simple, small, wild, and childlike beings. As a pure representation of the element of air, sylphs fly on the breeze and dance in dust storms. They're responsible for rustling leaves and branches, and they also make tumbleweeds race across plains. They fly alongside birds and surf the waves, kicking up foam and spray as they go. When the wind is still, the sylphs are resting and enjoying the bounty of the land. They wait to be inspired again, and once they are, they take flight.

Sylphs have the ability to influence the weather. They can be called upon to stir up a gentle wind. Sylphs can travel through solids and liquids to reach any destination. They feed on incense smoke and dance in the spirals. They adore music. You may have heard a sylph if you've ever heard a faint voice from nowhere or music in the wind from an unknown source.

Paracelsus, the Renaissance alchemist, was the first to use the word sylph for an air elemental. He said that sylphs were beautiful, humanoid creatures, and of all the elementals, they were the closest to humans because, like us, they also needed air. Other magicians postulated that sylphs could concentrate the air to create a body.

Sylphs are usually beneficial beings that assist with light magical practices and rituals. Due to their limited stature and nature, they aren't equipped for larger works of magic. Because sylphs have all the qualities of air, they're useful to call upon for magic involving communication, inspiration, creativity, imagination, and expansion. They can also help you get into a magical state of mind.

Fae/Faeries

The Fae, also known as faeries, are a collective of air entities with renowned stories from all over the world. They're synonymous with magic, sorcery, and enchantment, and it's said that they exist in the magical realm of air. They have even been described as having bodies made of congealed air, and some are devastatingly beautiful. The Fae are all sorts of sizes—anywhere from the size of a human to only a few inches tall. Though some of the Fae resemble humans, they have a much longer lifespan and they don't have human emotions.

Many faery tales originated several thousand years ago. In some of these stories, the Fae assist a good character who encounters undue difficulties. A good example of this is the story of Cinderella. In Perrault's 1697 version, a faery godmother uses glamour to allow Cinderella to appear as a princess and go to the royal ball. With the aid of the Fae, she wins the heart of the prince.

However, the Fae have also been known to play tricks and be malicious. One of the most widely known stories of this is the legend of the changeling. It was a common belief in many areas of the world that the Fae would swap unattended human babies for faery ones that cried all the time and were very different from the human children.

Due to this dual nature of the Fae, many people believed there were two different kinds of Fae—the seelie, or the good; and the unseelie, or the malicious. Although both could play pranks on people, the seelie were much less harmful.

Magically, the Fae are associated with the otherworld and the underworld, creativity, light, enchantment, glamor, imagination, agriculture, omens, animals, transformation, life, death, and manifestation. However, the Fae are a diverse group of spirits, many of whom are specific to certain regions or have special abilities. Before working with them magically, do some research to be aware of their qualities. For example, many of them will not come if summoned, and may take great offense at such commands. Research the ones you're interested in to ensure they're compatible with you and your magic.

Valkyries

Valkyries are the handmaiden spirits of Odin who fly over battlefields and ride alongside great warriors. The word *valkyrie* is derived from a combination of the old Norse words for *choose* and *battle-slain*. One of their roles is to pass judgment and choose who will die in battle.

Sometimes, valkyries are portrayed with large wings. Other times, they're depicted as warrior women riding horses. They're usually shown with spears, helmets, and armor, especially when they fight in battles to protect those they love. Upon the death of a warrior, valkyries ensure a safe journey to the afterlife by flying alongside the soul until they reach their final destination. They also serve ale and mead in Valhalla.

Mythical Locations

Mount Olympus

When the Olympian gods aren't on earth or in the underworld, they live in the cloudy realm of Mount Olympus. While an actual Mount Olympus exists as the tallest mountain in Greece, the home of the gods is thought to be far above the earth. It's a sublime place with no wind, rain, or snow. The sounds of Apollo's lyre echo throughout its halls, and the gods feast on ambrosia and nectar.

Castle in the Sky

In Traditional Witchcraft, when some Witches invoke air, they call upon a castle in the sky. This castle is the home of Tettans, the Celtic god of protection and hunting.

Asgard, Alfheim, and Nifelheim

In Norse mythology, three of the nine mythological worlds exist in the air. Asgard is the home of the gods. It exists in the sky, and Odin and Frigg rule over it. Inside of Asgard is the magnificent Valhalla, the afterlife world for fallen warriors. Asgard also contains the place known as Gimlé, the most beautiful location that has been reserved for only the best people who will survive the end of the world. Beside Asgard is Alfheim, the world of the elves of light, which are beautiful beings of good nature. These elves also live in two other realms of the skies that were abandoned by their original inhabitants. Nifelheim is another airy world of mist and fog, and it's the home of a dragon named Nidhug.

Shamballa

Hidden away in the Himalayan Mountains is the mythical realm of Shamballa. This is a place of peace, love, eternal youth, and vibrant health. It's mentioned in several ancient texts all over the region, and its myth goes back thousands of years.

Land of the Giants

In the ancient story of Jack and the Beanstalk, a boy receives magic beans, which are thrown out by his mother. Overnight, they grow to enormous sizes. He climbs the giant beanstalks to a world above, where giants dwelled in a land of plenty.

Faerie Realm

The Faerie realm is a plane of existence that lies parallel to ours. In this world live a multitude of spirits called the Fae. Many people have entered this realm by searching for enchanting music or by following a faery into it. The entry point could also be through the trunk of an old tree (usually an oak) or a faerie ring (a circle made of mushrooms). Some of the people who enter are never seen again, and others come back only to discover that a long time has passed. As in the underworld, it's wise to not consume any food or drink—those who do stay for an eternity.

Upperworld

The upperworld is a mythical realm above ours in energy. It's imbued with feelings of bliss. Mental and spiritual healing can occur here, and it's home to many spirits.

Sky Realm

The ancient Celts believed that the sky was a vast world where their deities resided in beautiful cities. The Turning Tower of the Heavens, or the *Caer Sidi*, is the residence of a raven god named Brān. The sky realm was also home to magical birds such as the Morrigan's ravens and crows.

Fly, My Pretties!

Although this chapter covers several myths, there's often a grain of truth in every story. For example, archeologists in New Zealand recently found evidence of an enormous bird that existed a thousand years ago, which would confirm the Maori legend of the giant eagle. Likewise, many magical practitioners work with sylphs, and people continue to encounter the Fae and wander in and out of the faerie realm to this day. Whether or not you come across these beings and places, they have a powerful draw on the imagination and the spirit. Use them as inspirations to foster your affinity for the magical element of air.

Chapter 3

AIR AND THE DIVINE

Air divinities can act as way-showers, especially in your air magic. They provide nuanced energy and assistance toward your goals. Nearly every historic civilization had deities who ruled the wind, air, storms, and skies. Many of these gods are credited with the creation of the universe, the earth, and human life. Sometimes, these gods were the utmost ruler of their pantheon and had more power and authority than most others combined. They clearly embody the physical and spiritual aspects of the element of air. This chapter also includes gods with the personal qualities of the element of air, including those ruling communication, intelligence, wisdom, justice, truth, and more.

Aeolus: Greek god of the wind. Commander of the four directional wind gods Boreas, Eurus, Notus, and Zephyrus.

Amaunet: Egyptian mother goddess of the invisible wind—a cosmic force of nature. From the dark nothingness, she created a wind so strong the universe and time were born. She breathed life into the world, creating plants, animals, and humanity.

Egyptian rulers called upon Amaunet to give them wisdom and good rulership. One of her animals is the hawk.

Amun: Egyptian god of the sun and air. In later periods, he is also credited with the creation of the world along with Amaunet. Together, they protect and regulate access to divine wisdom.

An *(also known as Anu)*: Sumerian god of the sky and heavens. He is the king of the gods and rules over his pantheon.

Apollo: Greek god of music, prophecy, knowledge, reason, and poetry.

Ara Tiotio: Maori god of tornados. He controls destructive winds and whirlwinds.

Astarte: Canaanite goddess of love and war known as the Queen of Heaven. Her favorite offering is incense.

Athena: Greek goddess of wisdom, reason, arts, crafts, and agriculture. Her name means air and mind of divinity. She often speaks to people in their visions and dreams. She invented the flute, and the owl is one of her animals. Her Roman equivalent is Minerva.

Au Set *(known as Isis by the Greeks)*: Egyptian mother goddess known as the Queen of Heaven. She is depicted with multicolored bird wings. Au Set is the oldest of the old and is the wise goddess from whom everything arose. She acts as a counselor and a diviner. She enforces the law and justice.

Ayida Wedo: Vodou spirit of the sky, fertility, and snakes. She is represented by the rainbow.

Baal: Egyptian god of thunder. His epithets include Lord of the Heavens and He Who Rides the Clouds.

Ba'al Hadad *(also known as Baalshamin)*: Canaanite god of thunder, lightning, the sky, and the air. He is the king of his pantheon.

Baba Yaga: Slavic Witch who flies through the air in a mortar and pestle. She is associated with death and has a hut perched on giant chicken legs.

Befana: Italian Witch who flies on a broomstick and delivers candy and presents to children just after the first of the year.

Bieg-Olmai *(also known as BiekaGalles)*: Lapp god who controls the wind and storms. From his underground cave, he shovels the winds in and out, deciding what season will happen and when. He helps sailors, especially when they're lost or in stormy weather. He is often featured on drums made of reindeer hide, some of which date back to 100 BCE.

Blodeuwedd: Welsh goddess of spring, flowers, and rebellion. She is associated with owls and wisdom.

Boreas: Greek god of the cold north wind and the bringer of winter.

Brān: Chief deity of the Celtic Tuatha Dé Dannan. He is a raven who resides in a watchtower called the Turning Tower of the Heavens, or the *Caer Sidi*, where he guards the cauldron of life.

Brigid: Celtic Tuatha Dé Dannan goddess of language, inspiration, and poetry, among other things.

Cailleach: Gaelic goddess of weather and winter who created mountains and valleys. She's portrayed as a hag with magical powers.

Cardea: ancient Roman goddess sometimes called the White Goddess. Cardea commands the four winds and she exists at the axis where they originate. She is also the goddess of hinges, and she can open doors that are closed and shut doors that are open. She also opens the ways to unseen forces, mysteries, and magic.

Cerridwen: Celtic goddess of intelligence, inspiration, knowledge, and rebirth.

Coelus: Roman sky god who is the equivalent of the Greek god Uranus.

Dogoda: Polish god of wind and compassion.

Ehécatl: Aztec god of unseeable, unknowable forces of love and passion. His name translates as four winds, or the winds from the four cardinal directions. He is one of the faces of Quetzal-coatl, the feathered serpent god.

Enlil: Sumerian god of air, breath, and wind. He is known as Lord Air.

Eurus: Greek god of the east wind, bringer of warmth and rain.

Feng Po Po: Chinese goddess also known as Madam Wind. She is the wise crone goddess of air, wind, and storms. She is depicted as an old woman who rides a tiger while carrying a sack of wind. She's responsible for all of the wind in the world, from calm breezes to foul storms. Through interpreting the winds, it is thought that one can discern her feelings.

Flora: Roman goddess of springtime and flowers.

Frigg: Norse goddess of wisdom and foresight. She's the Queen of Asgard and a skilled sorcerer who divines the future.

Fūjin: Japanese god of air and wind. He is known as the Prince of Long Breath.

Guabancex: Caribbean goddess of storms and hurricanes. She is called Lady of the Winds.

Hermes: Greek messenger of the Olympian gods. He flies as fast as thought with wings that adorn his sandals, helmet, and staff. Considered the smartest and most clever of his pantheon, Hermes routinely outsmarts the other gods simply because he can. He travels with the spirits of the dead to the underworld. He is said to be an enchanting musician and is credited with inventing the lyre and the shepherd's pipes. Mercury is his Roman equivalent.

Holle: European sky goddess known as Queen of the Witches, Queen of Heaven, and Our Lady. Holle is a magical shapeshifter who travels through the Milky Way galaxy in a wagon. She is often seen in whirlwinds and snowstorms. She assists women who wish for children by blowing spirits into their wombs.

Horus: Egyptian god of the sky depicted with a falcon head. He is known as The One Far Above, and he is a fierce protector and ruler.

Huracan (*also called Hu-Rakan*): Aztec/Caribbean god of storms, violent winds, and hurricanes.

Ilmarinen: Finnish and Russian god who created the sky and many other inventions. He can call upon the four winds.

Inanna: Sumerian goddess often depicted as a woman with bird wings and talons. She presides over trials of law and judgments. One of her animals is the owl. She later became associated with Ishtar, a similar Akkadian goddess.

Iris: Greek goddess of rainbows and messenger of the Olympian gods. This winged goddess has the ability to travel far and wide on the wind. She is considered the female counterpart of Hermes.

Janus: Roman god of beginnings and endings. Janus had two heads and could see into the past and into the future at the same time. He is also the god of motion, change, journeys, doorways, gates, and time.

Jupiter: Roman equivalent of the Greek god Zeus. Jupiter is the god of the sky and thunder, and he is the king of the gods in his pantheon. His temples had no roofs so the sky was visible at all times.

Kami-Shinatobe-no-Mikoto: Japanese goddess of the wind. She has distinctive horns and fangs.

Kami-Shinatsuhiko-no-Mikoto: Japanese wind god. When he was born, his breath was so strong that it dispersed the heavy clouds that covered the world and let the sunshine in.

Kari: Semang god who created the universe with one word. He rules law, judgment, and the wind. His voice ranges from booming thunder to the peaceful wind through the leaves. Kari is also the name of the Norse god of the wind.

La'amaomao: Hawaiian wind goddess. She rules over the thirty-two winds that blow over the island, which she keeps in a hollow gourd.

Legba: Haitian Vodou spirit associated with music, the moment before dawn, and communication with spirits. Legba knows all languages and carries messages to the gods and spirits. He is the first spirit honored before any ceremony, and he resides at the crossroads, a symbolic place of change and beginnings.

Libertas: Roman goddess of freedom. She was historically portrayed with a staff and a cap. Modern representations of her, like the Statue of Liberty, depict her with a torch and a book.

Lugh: Celtic solar deity associated with the sky. He also is a god of magic and poetry.

Mari: Spanish Basque creation goddess. Mari lives in a mountain cave and presides over the weather. She is known as Old Woman of the Mountain and is sometimes seen driving a cart in front of the full moon. When she creates a storm, a blessing is on its way to you, but only if you draw the blessing toward you. One of her animals is the raven. She often transforms herself into a bird to communicate with people.

Mnemosyne: Titan (Greek) goddess of memory.

Neith: Egyptian sky deity. Neith wove the world into being with a loom, and every day, she gives birth to the sun. She rules over the upper stratospheres and the universe. Neith is often referred to as a goddess, but some myths use androgynous language.

Ninlil: Sumerian goddess of the wind, grain, and pollination.

Njördr: Norse god of the wind and weather. He assists sailors with gusts and breezes.

Notus: Greek god of the hot south wind and bringer of storms.

Nut: Egyptian goddess of the portion of the sky closest to the earth. She protects the dead and is often depicted as a woman arching over the earth. She is the daughter of Shu, the god of air.

Obatalá: Haitin Vodoun supreme spirit. They are an androgynous creator deity who rules the skies, mind, intellect, and balance.

Odin *(also known as Woden)*: Norse god of the air and sky. Odin's breath gave life to the first humans. He is considered the wisest of all the Norse gods, and he passed that wisdom and poetry to humanity. One of his other names is Wanderer, as he travels throughout the many worlds. He's also a master of magic and inspiration. Odin has two ravens whose names mean thought and memory. He dresses in sky blue and rides a flying horse during the Wild Hunt. He resides in the afterlife world Valhalla with the souls of fallen warriors.

Olorún: Voodoo divine spirit known as the ruler of heavens. He breathed life into the first humans.

Ouranos: Titan (Greek) god of the sky. With Gaia, he created the earth. His Roman equivalent is Uranus.

Oyá: Haitian Vodou spirit of wind, weather, change, and magic. She guards cemeteries and the underworld and carries a sword of truth.

Persephone: Greek goddess of springtime and the Queen of the Underworld. When she travels from the underworld to the earth, the seasons change to springtime. The flowers bloom, releasing their aromas into the air.

Pheme: Greek goddess of fame. Her name translates to "speak." Pheme is personified as a winged goddess with a laurel wreath and a trumpet. She assists people in their quest to be renowned by furthering communication about them. However, she was a notorious gossip, and she lived up to her alternate name,

Rumor. Though her influence could aid someone, the gossip she repeated could likely ruin them. She is a messenger of Zeus.

Quetzalcoatl: Central American feathered serpent god of wind and rain. He created the world and books. He is known for his intelligence and wisdom.

Rajin: Japanese god of thunder.

Seshat: Egyptian goddess of writing and books. She also works with the dead.

Shu: Egyptian god of air and vital breath, or spirit.

Stribog: Slavic god of the winds, the sky, and air.

Themis: Titan (Greek) goddess of justice, law, and divine right. She holds a sword and a scale to weigh the actions of humanity. Her blindfold represents the concept that all people are equal, as she does not see wealth, class, or race. With her sword, she doles out justice to those who deserve it, cutting from some to compensate others, and severing life when it is owed. Themis sat on Zeus' throne beside him. Today, she is represented in many courtrooms. Her Roman equivalent is Justice.

Thor: Norse thunder god. He is an exacter of justice, striking down evil people and defending good people in their time of need. When Thor slams his hammer into an enemy, thunder roars out and lightning flashes. He's the strongest of the Norse gods and is able to destroy mountains. He travels across the sky in a chariot pulled by goats.

Thoth: Egyptian god of magic, wisdom, writing, law, and music. He is sometimes portrayed with an ibis head. Thoth wrote all of the divine texts, including the Book of the Dead.

Tyr: Norse god of justice and enforcer of the law.

Vejopatis: Lithuanian god of the wind. He is also known as the Master of Paradise.

Zephyrus: Greek god of the gentle west wind.

Zeus: Greek god whose titles include Lord of the Sky, Cloud Gatherer, and Thunderbolt Wielder. He is the father of the Olympian deities, and his strength is said to be greater than the combined power of all of the other Greek gods and goddesses. His animal is the eagle, and he also transforms into a swan. Although he is known for his many trysts, some of these stories may have been later additions to his myth.

Ritual for Protection
with the Elemental Guardians of Air

The Elemental Guardians of Air aren't thought of as gods, but they're very close to them, as they're far more powerful than most spirits. There are several names for the rulers, or royalty class, of the element of air, including the Guardians, the Watchers, the Keepers of the Watchtower, the Rulers, and Paralda. They're also thought of as angels, daimons, and enlightened spirits of the dead who have chosen to not reincarnate and instead choose to work with humans and their desires. They may be visible in their astral or energetic forms as somewhat human-shaped. Whatever they are, they're powerful, wise, primal, eternal, and pure energy. Magical practitioners often call upon them when casting a circle, for their benevolent and protective energy.

Invoking the Elemental Guardians of Air is an important part of many magical rituals. A lot of circles begin with someone calling upon them and continue by following through with the other elements in a clockwise manner. Likewise, when it's time to release the elements, the process goes backward from the way it was created, which means the Elemental Guardians of Air are the last to go.

There are a few reasons why the Elemental Guardians of Air are the first to come and the last to leave magical circles. As air spirits, they're initiators of new beginnings. They activate the circle and its magic. They facilitate connection with other spirits, including the other Elemental Guardians, our beloved dead, and deities. They give our tongues more grace so we can communicate with greater ease. They inspire us to speak the right words that will recreate the world as we speak them. When we release our magic into the world, they access the magical element of air and energetic portals that connect our words and vision to the rest of the world. They also protect magical workers from harm.

For all these reasons, the Elemental Guardians of Air act as initiatory guides for much magic, helping shape it with precisely the right intentions and spirits. Your ability to call upon them sets the tone for the airy aspects of the ritual and many other aspects as well. Starting with a strong and empowered summoning ensures greater all-around success for your magic.

However, you don't need a big ritual to call upon them. You can invoke them for small magical needs or whenever you need their assistance. They're great allies when you want protection, especially from spirits that may have hitchhiked into your house on a well-intentioned object. Because the Elemental Guardians of Air are beings of immense power, they will always come and assist you.

To call upon the Elemental Guardians of Air for protection, face east or another direction you associate with air, or simply face the sky. Clear your mind and take a deep breath in. Focus on the personal, magical, and physical qualities of air. Let your mind become clear and feel the energy of several air correspondences. Feel the lightness of the magical energy of air, the wind, and the vast sky. See air as an archetypal force of nature, as an element with more space than any other, as an elemental spirit, and as a vibration. With deep breaths, open yourself up to the energy. Feel your body become lighter as you embody the vibration of air. Align your body and your chakras to the frequency.

You don't have to speak out loud to invoke the Elemental Guardians of Air; however, because air is the element of communication, it's fitting to use the power of the spoken word.

Guardians of the Element of Air,

Spirits of the East,

I call upon you to protect my sacred circle.

Lend your wisdom, your clear thinking,

Your ability to discern and decide,

And your connection with the spirit realms.

Guide my words and elevate my magic.

Guardians of Air, welcome!

Wait to feel their presence before proceeding. You may feel a chill or a subtle energy shift. You may also feel a presence in the room. Perform your magical workings. When your work is done, release them.

Guardians of the Element of Air,

Spirits of the East,

Thank you for assisting in my magical work

And for protecting my sacred circle.
I give thanks for your wisdom, insights, and gifts.
Until we meet again, farewell.

• • • •

The Gender Evolution of Air

Elliot Director, PhD, is a fat, queer dad and Witch living with his partner, child, and cat in northeast Ohio. He writes and teaches about gender-inclusive, ethical, and anti-racist witch-craft. Elliot also writes as a guest contributor on Patheos on his blog *Beyond Binary Witchcraft*.

THE TRADITION OF four or five classical elements—air included—has a long history, from the five great elements discussed in the Vedas to the four elements in Buddhist philosophy to Greek antiquity, where they were again identified as earth, air, fire, and water. The Greeks asserted elemental correspondences regarding temperature; those elements that were associated with heat were the elements of air and fire. Perceived as "active," both elements were identified as masculine.

Later, in the nineteenth and early twentieth centuries, early occultists of the Hermetic Order of the Golden Dawn developed or documented extensive practices and theories regarding magic, part of which included these teachings that air and fire were the masculine or "male" elements because they were both active and projective (versus water, for example, which was seen as passive and receptive). Later occultists, among them Gerald Gardner, relied in part upon these teachings to develop their own theories about the relationship between gender, the elements, and magic.

This binary ideology became entrenched within the foundations of Wicca and Witchcraft.

With the emergence of Dianic witchcraft and the increasingly public presence of LGBTQ Witches and Wiccans in the 1970s and 1980s, some began to challenge the highly gendered, binary framework that had dominated established witchcraft philosophy. By the late 1990s and early 2000s, Witches had begun to openly challenge the practice of gendering everything from tools to roles to the elements themselves. Toward the end of the 2010s, a surge of scholarship, theology, and activism resulted in an approach to witchcraft that decenters a gendered component to the elements. Such approaches create space for practitioners to see correlations between multiple gendered aspects and the elements, or to shift entirely away from thinking about the elements in relation to any particular gendered energy (along with many other aspects of witchcraft).

These days, a Witch or pagan might welcome a warm summer wind as an inherently feminine blessing from a femme goddex, or call upon the powers of air for their blessing in writing or with creativity, acknowledging these as primal experiences that are both active and passive. For many, the intellectual and creative process emerges not just from the hot, active spark of imagination, but also from the cool, mellow winds of reflection, both of which are invaluable gifts that may cause us to ask for the blessings of air.

Elliot Director

• • • •

Meditative Journey to an Air Deity's Temple

Deep within our minds, we have vast universes and landscapes. There are wild places like deserts, forests, and beaches, as well as familiar places like your childhood home. Any location that you've been to or imagined is contained within your mind. These archetypical places represent bits and pieces of ourselves at various ages and levels of consciousness, and they can be visited during meditation for healing and self-actualization. This meditative journey could be taken while reading this book, or you could record it and play it back to yourself.

Begin by deepening your breathing. Fill your diaphragm with air and release it entirely. Inhale and continue your long, big breaths. Pause between your inhalations and exhalations to hold your breath for a moment. Go ahead and let your thoughts go. Feel yourself sink down into a beautiful trance state of mind.

Think of an air deity you'd like to encounter. Speak their name in your mind. Envision what they look like to you. Call to mind their symbols and feel their energy. Slowly, shift your energy to be more like theirs. Feel the change and transformation within you as you shift your cells to their frequency.

Now, imagine you are standing in front of a giant, old tree that has branches that rise up high into the clouds. The trunk is wide, and as you gaze at the bark, you notice a doorway there. Allow the door to open, and take a few steps forward until you're inside the tree trunk. Instantly, feel yourself lifted up and floating, as if an elevator is transporting you up, higher and higher. As you float upward, speak the deity's name again to yourself.

Soon, you notice an opening in the trunk just above you. Float higher and step through the doorway and out. You find yourself just outside of the temple of the air deity you're calling upon. Notice what the ground looks like. Look at how the temple looks. Notice the weather, the wind, the colors here, the time of day, and the smells. If it feels right, step inside the temple. Look at the decorations inside, and at the altar set up inside there. Look around at the views from that location. Explore the temple and really feel the energy and presence of the deity there.

When you are ready to meet with the deity, speak their name within your mind and ask them to come. When they arrive, notice everything about them. Tell them your name and why you have called upon them. You may ask for a blessing, ask for assistance, or give them an offering such as incense, which you can light with your imagination. Ask if they have a message for you and listen to what they say. If you wish, have a conversation or simply commune with their energy.

When it's time to go, give gratitude to the deity and the magical place, and bid them farewell. Return to the outside of the temple and find your way to the tree trunk with the doorway. Go inside and feel a gentle fall as you float back down, down, down, all the way until your feet touch the earth. Allow the door of the tree trunk to open, and step outside.

With a sharp inhalation, call your thoughts back to you. Stretch and wiggle your fingers and toes to help you return to your body. You may want to write down your encounter with the deity and what the temple looked like. Through meditation, you're able to access this air temple and/or deity at any time. If you had a good experience, consider visiting them regularly to learn from them and receive their counsel.

O, Mighty Deities of Air!

Whether these air deities rule the wind, justice, thought, creation, storms, or the sky, they exemplify the divine powers of air. Their wondrous myths inspire us to find them in the world. If you can find them in their natural habitat, as the ancient pagans did, you'll be closer to them and their beneficial presences. The next time you feel a breeze brush over your skin, or you feel inspiration course through you, or you feel a sense of justice stir within you, ask yourself if it's one of these deities. If so, consider working with them more often to gain their insights and wisdom.

Chapter 4

SACRED AIR SITES

There are several places in the world that are sacred sites for the element of air. At some of these locations, the veils may be thinner and the air can feel thick with spirits. At other places, our personal connections with the element of air are highlighted. This list of sacred air sites includes both tangible and intangible places—everything from mountain ranges to the resting places of the dead to the shrine in your living room. When we celebrate the influences these air sites have on us, we more easily draw upon the magnificent powers of air whenever we wish.

Air Power Locations

Sometimes when I arrive at a place, I can feel strong air energy there. It's as if a magical wind is blowing and stirring my soul. Whether this sensation is from the wind, beautiful aromas, or a spiritual setting, there's no doubt that these places are special. Many of these sacred locations of air are liminal, meaning between two or more different places, such as the seashore. Others highlight the personal aspects of air, such as universities.

This list contains some of the airiest locations in and out of this world. As you read about these sacred air sites, take a moment to imagine you're there. Feel the energy and strengths of the element of air. Channel their powers within you and envision how you might use them the next time you visit these places.

These airy locations are very different from one another, but they all have one thing in common: air power in abundance. When you need more air energy in your life, use them to your advantage. Plan a trip to visit one of them. Upon arrival, take a moment to feel the air energy there and honor it. Ask yourself which air aspects these places spark within you—the personal, the spiritual, or the physical? Or perhaps a combination? Take advantage of the bountiful air energy by opening yourself to change in the manner you wish most, and breathe in the beneficial energies.

The Sky

It's easy to gaze up at the vast sky and feel awe at the nearly limitless scene that stretches from one end of visibility to the next. The enormity of the sky is related to the expansive and uplifting powers of air—the mere act of looking up makes some people feel more positive.

Another airy aspect of the sky is change—this is most evident in the weather, which is bound to shift from one moment to the next. The sky also carries the powers of communication. It's the perfect medium through which messages travel, whether it's a spoken word, an email, or your magic. Travel also takes place in the sky, whether it's a bird or an airplane. Lastly, the elevated power of air is demonstrated by the great, unreachable heights of the skies.

With all of these immense air powers, it's no wonder that the sky is connected with spirituality and divinities. There are countless deities of the skies, and it's home to many gods as well. In fact, there are so many deities who call the sky home that it's often venerated as "the heavens."

Elevated Locations

Mountains and hills are closer to the sky than the land surrounding them—as such, they're associated with the powers of the air, sky, and earth. These liminal places are highly spiritual and often quite windy too. People who work with deities of wind and air would benefit from practice there; however, all kinds of deities are associated with elevated locations.

The Canaanite people erected temples on hilltops for Astarte, the goddess known as the Queen of Heaven. They added tall pillars to their temples, which elevated their divinity even higher. Likewise, the temples of Athena and Nike in Athens also have an elevated worship. They're located at the highest point in the city on a rocky outcropping known as the Acropolis. The temple to Apollo and the Oracle at Delphi were also situated high up on the slopes of Mount Parnassus. Other elevated pagan places include the Temple of Mars in the mountains of Montmartre and, of course, Mount Olympus, the home of the Greek gods.

Another connection among mountains, divinity, and spirits is the fact that some Witches use them as astral meeting spots for the sabbaths. They congregate at the full moon in spectral form along with other spirits and deities. Witches may have preferred these remote locations due to their liminality, inaccessibility from others, and also as an easy point of reference.

Human-made Structures

The enormous height of towers, skyscrapers, windmills, and statues that rise high into the air can be breathtaking. They demonstrate the elevated character of air. Many of them are zeniths of mental powers such as logic and reason too, especially considering how much thinking, planning, and calculating were necessary to construct them. Some in this list are also spiritual in nature.

One of the amazing examples of this category is the Russian statue *The Motherland Calls*. Picture a 279-foot statue of a woman in Grecian robes holding a sword high in the air and reaching another arm out behind her. Her mouth is open as if she has a lot to communicate. This statue serves as a memorial for the dead—beneath her feet lie the remains of almost thirty-five thousand unidentified Soviet soldiers.

Some of the best structures permit you to climb their stairs or take an elevator so you too can be closer to the sky. If you've never visited a skyscraper, a watchtower, or even a prairie tower to a high floor and looked out over the landscape below, I highly encourage you to do so. For many people, the feeling of elevation and objectivity below is quite intoxicating. Other places to do this include the Central American pyramids, the Eiffel Tower, the St. Louis Gateway Arch, the Seattle Space Needle, the Tower of Pisa, Machu Picchu, the Egyptian pyramids, or the Statue of Liberty, which was modeled after the Roman goddess Libertas.

Windy Places

There are several parts of the world where the wind is blowing more often than not. Windy places represent air's qualities of movement, change, and action. To catch a good breeze, visit a beach or a large lake—wind is generated at these locations when energy is transferred between the water and the land. Other windy places include hills and mountains, as mentioned above, and the area between 5 and 30 degrees latitude north and south, where the trade winds blow.

Schools, Colleges, Universities, and Libraries

Areas of higher learning reflect the mental aspects of air. There's so much learning, intelligence, communication, discernment, and logic there. There may even be creativity and spirituality, depending on the buildings and their uses.

Courtrooms

Places of law evoke air's aspects of communication, discernment, and judgment. The principles of logical arguments, justice, and the law are also empowered. Many courtrooms contain images or statues of the goddess Justice/Themis, who is often portrayed wearing a blindfold and holding a sword and scales.

Concert Halls and Music Venues

Musical performance spaces are considered air locations due to the way sound and music reverberate through the air. If these places were created with acoustics in mind, sounds from the stage can be transmitted to reach the very last row in the audience. These places embody the creative, logical, and imaginative aspects of air.

Airports

There's so much change, movement, and travel at airports that they're immersed in the energy of air. Flights launch people high into the sky, even if it's just for a short time. Airports highlight the elevated, traveling, and changeable energies of air. An airplane trip can be a wonderful location to practice some subtle air magic, especially if you have a window seat to look out at the clouds and the land far below.

Spiritual Centers

Spiritual places such as temples, churches, sacred groves, and mosques are connected with the element of air due to their divine connection. Ones that have bell towers and spires that rise high into the sky have the elevated correspondence of air. They may have additional air magic if they use flowers, incense, bells, or music in their ceremonies.

Yoga and Meditation Centers

At yoga and meditation centers, there's a huge focus on the breath. The best yoga centers encourage connecting the breath with the body's movements, which is the meaning of the Hindu word *yoga*. This meditative breath connects the spirit and the mind, which enables a greater sense of objectivity and a feeling of freedom. If spirituality, incense, and sound or music are incorporated into their practices, the level of air energy is increased.

The Resting Places of the Dead

Wherever the deceased are venerated, the spiritual facet of the element of air is present. The resting places of the dead include cemeteries, graveyards, crypts, mausoleums, tombs, niches, columbaria, and shrines. Many of these places were built on higher grounds, which adds the elevation aspect of air as well. Elevated locations were chosen because those places are less likely to flood compared to valleys, and also due to the ancient association of high places with spirits, the sky, and divinity. One example of such a gravesite is the Neolithic burial mound in Newgrange, Ireland, which stands 115 feet high.

Among the most famous resting places for the dead, albeit underground, are the Catacombs of Paris. In these tunnels and rooms, there are countless artistic formations of human bones and skulls.

The Elemental Realm of Air

This elemental plane is where spirits reside, and where we, too, can fly through the air astrally. This sacred space overlaps with ours in many ways, but it's not restricted by the physics of our world. The veil that separates our world from the elemental realm of air is thinner in some places, such as in ancient stone circles. Likewise, during certain times, such as Samhain and Beltane, the veil becomes thinner for everyone all around the world. The elemental realm of air may be where the gods reside too, or they may live in a realm just beyond it. It demonstrates the spiritual aspect of air as well as the power of thought.

Magical Circles

Whenever we cast a magical circle, we create a spiritual space between the worlds that has never existed before. In these liminal locations, we become intensely connected with the magical element of air. Our thoughts and words have much more power there than anywhere else. The spirits whom we invite to our circles listen to the words we speak and assist us with communicating our desires far and wide. We can also use the elemental realm of air to transmit our thoughts and desires to the world without any assistance from spirits.

Besides the spiritual aspect of air, there are many other powers of air in magical circles. It's where we create change in our lives. Tools of air are often used there, most notably to cast these circles, such as the athame and the wand, though spirits may be used as well. Circles are also one of the best places to practice visionary and divinatory arts.

Air Shrines and Altars

A great way to connect with the element of air more often is to create places for it in your home or yard. These could take many forms, each of which has its own beneficial aspects. Set up your air shrine or altar in whichever direction makes the most sense for your practice. Be sure to use items you associate with air to stir the magic within you.

Air Shrine

One of the best ways to connect with the element of air is to set up an air shrine. Generally speaking, a shrine is any spiritual space associated with a deity, a spirit, your ancestors, or several spirits or deities. They can be any size from a small box to a space within a room or an entire room. Think of shrines as homes for the energy, deity, or spirit. Shrines are often decorated with art, whether it's a portrayal such as a Buddha statue at a meditation shrine; or a symbolic token, such as a key for Hekate. Other objects that evoke the essence of the spirit, such as photographs or heirlooms, may also be placed there.

Shrines are often called altars, but they're different—shrines are more like magical-feeling places where you commune with energy, and altars are the place where your magical work happens. Common activities at shrines include devotional activities, meditation, prayer, and communion. You can make offerings in the form of flowers, food, or incense.

Setting up an air shrine is a great way to become more in touch with the element of air. It may be as complicated or simple as you wish. If you prefer a minimalist approach, use only one or two representations, such as a yellow watercolor painting or a mobile. One benefit of these simple shrines is that artwork is a normal thing to have in plain sight. This is nice if outsiders visit often or if you share a space with other people.

Of course, you could go the opposite way and use a lot of objects. My air shrine consists of the top two shelves of a bookcase with artwork of owls and the goddess Athena, a vase with feathers, incense, a censer, white and blue candles, bells, butterfly wings, and essential oils. I also keep clear quartz, apophyllite, amethyst, and moldavite crystals there. All of these things represent what air feels like to me.

Consider whether you might want to place your shrine outdoors. This would be especially suitable if it's dedicated to a deity of weather or wind, spirits of air, or the Fae. Hang weatherproof items such as chimes, ribbons, and figurines in the air to make it special.

Another alternative is a window shrine to the element of air. Attach ribbons, bells, stained glass figures, figurines, prisms, and other décor from the curtain rod to create a light, airy feeling. Use a semi-transparent curtain to be able to see sunlight or moonlight through it. Window shrines are especially nice in windows that face the direction you associate with air.

Air Represented on the Main Altar

Your main altar is the place for your primary magical workings. It's often decorated for the season, holiday, or a specific ritual. The main altar also contains the magical tools used in the majority of rituals. In this way, it acts as a worktable for your magic. The air tools include incense, the athame, and/or the wand. Find more information on those in chapters 5 and 6.

Your main altar could be situated in the central area of your ritual space; however, if you have a special affinity to air, or you want to use it to work air magic, position it at whichever direction you associate with the element of air. Placing it there increases your personal communication and helps with spirit work.

Air Altar

On the shelf just below my air shrine, I have a dedicated area that I use as an altar for the element of air. It's a convenient place to work when I want to do air magic and not use any of the other elements. I also use it to store my air tools. Keeping my incense and athame there clears up space on the main altar for other things. It prevents me from having to move them back and forth too.

I use this altar to store all of my air magic. It just feels right to keep certain things there, such as spell jars for communication or charm bags for change. These magical items add to the unique energy of the air altar, and all of them can be recharged at the same time with incense.

Tap into the energy of your air altar whenever you need it. Simply light some incense, call upon whichever airy aspect you need, and draw energy from it with a deep breath.

Your air altar doesn't have to be as complicated as mine. Yours should reflect your unique personality and your magic. Do whatever feels right for your magical needs and the space.

Incense Table

In some cultures, incense is stored and burned at its own dedicated table. Having a special table for your incense means that you'll always have everything on hand. Another great thing about incense tables is that the embers are more out of reach.

Consider using a table that's waist-high for ease of lighting incense. Choose one with shelves or drawers to store your items. Stock your incense table with lighters, various kinds of incense, incense charcoal, tongs, censers, a cauldron or a heat-safe bowl, and anything else you might need, including something to safely catch messy ashes. This makes them less of a fire hazard and much easier to clean up, compared to an altar cloth or a table. Place your incense table in the direction you associate with air, or set it up near the entrance to the sacred space to instantly create a spiritual mindset.

Ritual to Dedicate an Air Altar or Shrine

Whenever you create a new sacred place in your home, it's a good idea to have a light ritual to align it with your purposes. You don't need to cast a circle for this. All you need to do is tell it what you desire. This ritual calls upon the Guardians of the Element of Air for protection and to charge the altar with a purpose. Feel free to adapt the words to suit your dedication.

Guardians of the Element of Air,
I ask you to bless this altar/shrine

placed in the east, location of the rising sun and moon,

representing the beginning and the light,

the breath and the mind, wisdom and communication.

Upon this altar/shrine lies the feather of an owl,

most sacred animal to wise Athena,

bringer of wisdom and craft.

I burn this incense to honor you and to beseech you

to bless this altar/shrine of air,

and all air magic performed here.

May I find elevation, discernment, ideas, and insights,

and so much more, now and always.

So may it be.

Light some incense and waft it over the altar or shrine. Meditate and commune with the energy present until the incense burns out completely. Thank the spirits and bid them farewell.

• • • •

The Element of Air as an Altar

Laura Tempest Zakroff is a professional artist, author, dancer, designer, and Modern Traditional Witch. She is the author of the best-selling books *Weave the Liminal* and *Sigil Witchery*, as well as *The Witch's Cauldron*, and the co-author of *The Witch's Altar*. Laura blogs for *Patheos* and *Witches & Pagans*, contributes to *The Witches' Almanac, Ltd.*, and edited *The New Aradia: A Witch's Handbook to Magical Resistance*. Visit her at www.LauraTempestZakroff.com.

THERE ARE ALTARS to the elementals, and then there is using an element as an altar. The former falls under the shrine category, as the focus is to honor the elements and their related spirits. The latter focuses on the element being an altar itself—the crux where sacrifices and offerings are made and transformed.

The element of air is the miracle of the unseen and its definitive effect on the tangible. It is the essence of all invisible phenomena, explained or otherwise, that we can clearly see interacting with the world around us. We don't see wind, but we feel it and see it move the grass and the leaves on the trees. We know that air gives us life—it is what we breathe, and it's an integral part of our existence. We can't see it, but we know it's there by its effect on us. It is essential for all of the other elements to take place.

As an altar, air is a vehicle and a dispenser. It carries the smoke of what we set on fire and the plumes of fragrant incense up to the sky and heavens. Many cultures believe that gods, spirits, and ancestors feed upon the smoke of offerings and the aroma of incense and oils. Air, as wind, also blows the particles of burnt offerings and ash to the four corners of the earth. We can also use our own breath as a sacrifice to give of ourselves, our essence. Breath can also be infused with an offering as well as cleanse and direct with it.

It's relatively easy to use air as an altar. You can burn incense, anoint with essential oils (apply, or use an oil or wax warmer, which spreads the scent in a room), use an aromatic spritzer or cleansing spray, or simply apply focused breath onto an object or space. These all work fairly well in indoor spaces, but be sure to read about things to be cautious about. In outdoor spaces, if you're looking to harness the power of the wind, it may take a bit more planning and luck. You'll need to see where the wind is coming from and make sure the place you are working in is accessible to it.

A chant for using air as an altar:

> *Spirit of Air, Giver of Breath*
>
> *Weaver of Wind, Essence of Sky*
>
> *Take with you my sacred offering*
>
> *Upon your wings it now flies!*
>
> *Laura Tempest Zakroff*

• • • •

Sacred Air

No passage about sacred air sites would be complete without mentioning the most miraculous place of all for the element of air—your body! Your breath, mind, and spirit are housed in an amazing organism. Your body is a powerful entity that facilitates your use of air magic. If you bring a sense of wonder about the element of air with you wherever you go, you'll always be at a sacred air site.

PART
2

WORKING WITH THE ELEMENT OF AIR

To practice magic is to be a quack;
to know magic is to be a sage.

—ÉLIPHAS LÉVI

Chapter 5

THE ELEMENT OF AIR IN MAGIC

Since the magical element of air was conceived, philosophers, alchemists, and modern-day writers associated certain qualities with it. These are known as correspondences, and they include symbols, cardinal directions, times, seasons, planets, and much more. Each item in this chapter exemplifies air and adds a specific energy to your air magic. Some of them resonate more with the personal element of air, some the physical, and some the magical. Many are a combination of two or all three. This chapter goes deeper into a true understanding of the element of air.

Axiom of Air

The axiom of air is *to know*: the mental prowess of air is evident in the desire to learn and fully understand. This phrase reveals the willingness to research, seek answers, hypothesize, experiment, and solve problems. Any quest for true knowledge accepts that there may be great wins and successes as well as trials and failures, for only through facing challenges can we gain the wisdom of experience.

Symbol

Air is represented in alchemical texts as an upright triangle with a horizontal line through it. It looks like a combination of the capital letter A and a triangle, the chemical symbol for change. These reflect air's primary nature (the first letter of the alphabet) and its tendency to transform.

Gesture

In some traditions, when air is called upon in magical workings, it's represented by one hand in the air with the fingers spread wide, as if to catch the breeze.

Energy

The energy of air is active, initiative, dynamic, focused, direct, capable, mental, logical, clear-seeing, clear-thinking, and intellectual. Air is always moving, traveling, and churning, much like thoughts in an inquisitive mind. It's flexible, fast, new, changeable, unstable, and communicative. Just thinking about the energy of air should feel fresh and invigorating. Air is usually thought of as the lightest element. Although many ancient philosophers associated air with being cold, it's more common nowadays to see it associated with warmth. Air is also associated with moisture.

Direction

The ancient Greek alchemist Zosimos was the first known person to associate air with a direction—south. However, the direction most associated with air these days is east, the location of the rising sun and moon. This is likely due to a correspondence from the Enochian Magicians from the 1500s, which influenced the Golden Dawn and contributed to many of Wicca's traditions.

However, other people use other directions for air. For example, Traditional Witches associate it with the north and the season of winter. Many people in the southern hemisphere have been known to opt for whichever directional associations make the most sense based on their landscapes.

Time of Day

Air is associated with dawn, early morning, the moment before the sun rises, sunrise, and the rising sun. These moments are considered the birth of the day and the liminal change between darkness and light. The energy of air begins the day and gives everything a fresh start. It has the powers of new beginnings, hope, ability, wakefulness, light, and purpose. In Mesopotamia, spells were written with the rising of the sun, connecting language, the direction east, the sun, and magic.

Season

Air is traditionally associated with springtime. This is the season of new beginnings, fresh starts, and hope. It's when flowers once again grace the earth to perfume the air after the long, cold winter. Springtime is when many animals give birth to new life. It's also a natural time of purification, detoxification, and spring cleaning. The magical energies associated with springtime are awakenings, fertility, healing, magic, new beginnings, beauty, rebirth and renewal, hope, youth, and light.

Moon Phase

Many people link air to the waxing crescent and first quarter moon phases. This is likely due to the active aspects of air as well as its tendency to expand.

Senses

Smell: The sense of smell is one of the strongest senses, and it links the breath with the mind. Whenever aromas are inhaled, they travel directly into the limbic system, the part of the brain responsible for intuition and gut reactions. As such, smells evoke deep memories and emotions.

Hearing: Waves of sound travel through the air as audible frequencies. Sounds can evoke strong feelings—hearing a song from a certain era of your life transports you back to your mindset at that age.

Colors

Many different colors are associated with air, probably more than any other element. These colors are used to represent the element of air in art, altar cloths, candles, and magical workings.

Yellow: This is a common choice, as the color of the sun is perceived as yellow. Any color from a pale yellow to a golden hue can be used.

Silver: The silvery color of the moon is a beautiful option if you prefer moon magic and do magical works at night.

White: White is the color of neutral light and clouds.

Blue and purple: These colors represent the throat chakra and the third eye chakra. Blue is also the color of a cloudless sky.

Humor

The ancient Greek physician Hippocrates associated fluids with the elements: he associated air with blood because they are both hot and wet. This was a very astute insight, especially considering that, with each breath, oxygen molecules pass into tiny capillaries in the lungs, which transfer the oxygen molecules into the bloodstream. The body's cardiovascular system then spreads the oxygen throughout the entire body. Blood also transports carbon dioxide, a gaseous waste product, to the lungs, where we exhale it out.

Astrology

Some magical practitioners watch the stars so they can work their magic in alignment with the energies that are naturally available at that time. Whenever the sun, moon, or a planet is in an air sign, you'll get an extra dose of air energy. Special times for air magic include new moons in air signs, eclipses in air signs, conjunctions of two or more planets in air signs, or when air planets are 60 degrees apart.

Zodiac Signs Associated with Air

Gemini: This communicative sign has many airy traits, including the ability to talk with anyone about anything. It promotes a glib, fun energy, and has the power of twins and duality. Gemini is a mutable sign—it makes transitions well and helps others bridge gaps in thinking and feeling. When it's aspected well, Gemini is friendly, comedic, and brilliant. When aspected poorly, it's divided, contrary, fickle, and cutting. It's the airy aspect of Mercury. Use it in magic for adaptability, intelligence, wit, mental powers, change, relationships, and communication.

Libra: This sign of love, harmony, art, and beauty loves to entertain and flatter. Libra is a cardinal sign, meaning that it's good for starting or initiating projects. When aspected well, Libra is adaptable, friendly, charming, social, and graceful. When aspected poorly, it's indecisive, easily compromised, and codependent. Libra is the airy aspect of Venus. Use it in magic for balance, attraction, romance, relationships, cooperation, truth, beauty, justice, fairness, harmony, and grace.

Aquarius: This air sign is a humanitarian and an idealist. It's naturally detached from the world and identifies more with the stars, but at the same time, it desires a better society for all. Aquarius is a fixed sign, which means it's good for sustaining energy and carrying it forward. When aspected well, Aquarius is imaginative, bright, and idealistic. When aspected poorly, it's spacy, aloof, and alien. It's the airy aspect of Uranus. Use it in magic for community, creativity, intuition, wisdom, spirituality, hope, independence, charity, intelligence, healing, and peace.

Planets Associated with Air

Mercury: This fast-moving planet is associated with the god Hermes. Its strengths include communication, intelligence, creativity, the mind, adaptability, speed, inspiration, magic, business and money, omens, the underworld, wisdom, and travel.

Jupiter: Jupiter is known as the gas giant, and it's the largest planet in our solar system. It's associated with the element of air due to its connection with Zeus. Its traits include expansiveness, wealth, success, power, luck, generosity, intuition, leadership, opportunities, the mind, and spirituality.

Uranus: Uranus is one of the outermost planets in our solar system. It's named after Ouranos, the Greek god of the skies. This planet corresponds with radical change, inspiration, freedom, intuition, power, ambition, and motivation.

Personal Qualities of Air

It can be useful to think about what a strong personal association with the element of air looks like. Someone with positive qualities and traits of air would have these abilities:

Communication: Anyone who easily exchanges ideas and information has the gift of communication. They express themselves effectively and concisely in their writing, speaking, sign language, and other forms of communication.

Intelligence: People who are intelligent value the learning experience, research, thinking, understanding, and the application of those abilities. This includes being able to concentrate and memorize important information.

Discernment: In the Age of Information, you can learn nearly anything, but discernment is necessary to know what's fact and what's fiction. Discernment could be interpreted as the ability to use judgment, analyze information, and think critically. This quality gets to the heart of the matter.

Vision: The ability to imagine, visualize, invent, dream, and create is highly underrated. Vision helps leaders rally people behind a cause. It can also lead us down new paths we haven't explored before.

Wisdom: the knowledge that comes from trial and error, learning lessons, and experience is known as wisdom. It's related to intelligence, discernment, spirituality, and memory.

Magical Air Tools

The tools of air are used to cleanse, change, cut, focus, and communicate. Although tools aren't necessary for witchcraft, they're quite useful. For example, I can't imagine chopping vegetables without a knife or cleaning the floor with my hands instead of a broom. Tools have a long history of magical use for a reason—they work.

Athame, Dagger, Knife, or Sword

In witchcraft, knives are primarily used to perform energetic cuttings. They are used to cut through the fabric of the world to create a magical circle. They're also used to cut energetic cords that connect people to places or things. Another use is to banish spirits, summon spirits, and carve symbols and sigils in the air.

Knives have protective air properties as well—there are a few anecdotes that support this. Knives are traditionally made of a metal such as steel, which contains a large amount of iron. You may have heard of the legend that the faery folk don't like iron or steel. The knife's ability to cut through the element of air may be the reason why. Likewise, a circle cast with a knife keeps out spirits who are not invited, as they are not able to cross through the circle.

Magic Wand

Wands have a long history of magical use. One of their primary functions is to raise energy, direct spirits, and facilitate the flow of a ritual. Like a conductor with an orchestra of musicians, someone who wields a wand can use it to project their mentality on the spirits present in a ritual. Wands are used to whip up the air in a magical circle, which excites the spirits and increases the amount of energy present. This coordinates the energy and allows the ritual to move together to culminate and intensify with all participants feeling bonded as one.

Wands are also used to transmit one's energy into the world. Whenever I raise a wand to the elemental realm of air, I imagine it touching the invisible web that connects everything in the universe. Wands conduct our energy and send our thoughts out along those strands to transmit our desires. This is especially useful for summoning spirits that can assist with your magic.

Some other common uses of magic wands include calling upon the elemental guardians at each cardinal direction, casting circles, banishing spirits, and directing energy into objects.

Do Wands And Knives Actually Correspond with Fire?

Depending on the tradition, both wands and knives are said to correspond with fire, not air. As it turns out, there are compelling arguments for each designation.

Ancient witchcraft traditions associated wands with fire and knives with air. Look no further than the tarot deck to see this association. Enochian alchemists of the late medieval era and the Hermetic Order of the Golden Dawn also used these same corresponding energies. However, Scott Cunningham, one of the foremost Wiccan authors of the twentieth century, reversed these correspondences, and associated wands with air and athames with fire.

We can evaluate each tool based on its natural associations with air. Consider the argument that wands correspond with air—it's easy to imagine the wand as a tree branch, high above the ground and blowing in the wind. Birds may have rested on it, and they may have even constructed a nest there.

Now, let's consider the argument that knives correspond with air. Knives slice through the air sharper than wands ever could. The sharp, cutting ability of the knife relates to the air qualities of discernment and logic. Similarly, swords are associated with air deities of logic and wisdom, such as Themis and Justice.

Both arguments are compelling in their own right, but there's a third option—what if wands and knives both correspond with the energy of air? It's possible to think of their individual air aspects when you use them. Use both tools and ascertain which one(s) feels like air to you. If you're still uncertain, simply use incense or another magical tool to represent air.

Staff

Staffs could be thought of as longer versions of wands with a few extra properties. In addition to all of the wand's uses, the staff is used to call upon the underworld and the upperworld. It acts as a conduit between the two or three worlds, allowing that energy to flow into the person who wields it. In this way, it acts as an *axis mundi* or tree of the world. Staffs can also be used to draw a magical circle in the soil or sand.

Magical Broom or Besom

Magical brooms, also known as besoms, aren't usually associated with any element; however, they could be considered air tools because they're used to sweep negative and stagnant energy from the air. Some of the besoms historically used for cleansing purposes have air correspondences. For example, the Romans used brooms made of vervain to sweep the air around their temples and altars. Using a specific plant in a besom adds that energy to the cleansing. Besoms and brooms are also associated with astral projection and magical flight.

Pen and Paper

Several ancient cultures believed in the power of the written word. Ancient Egyptians believed that the written word (and image) affected reality. They wrote down things that were in power, which reaffirmed the power even more. The word *grammar*, meaning rules of language, has magical roots—it's a descendent from the Egyptian word *grimoire*, a book of magical spells.

If you want to increase the power of your written words, use more powerful affirmations in rituals and write them down. You can also commit more time to your journal or Book of Shadows. Take your time writing things down to capture the essence of your rituals and practices. Organize your entries so you can go back, read them, and not only make sense of them, but also gain wisdom about how your magic was woven into the greater picture.

• • • •

Air and the Tarot

Phoenix LeFae is a restless seeker of knowledge. She is an initiate in the Reclaiming Tradition of Witchcraft, the Avalon Druid Order, and Gardnerian Wicca. She is a hoodoo practitioner, professional Witch, and the owner of the esoteric Goddess shop, Milk & Honey, in Sebastopol, CA. She has had the pleasure of teaching and leading ritual across the United States, Canada, and Australia. Phoenix's books include *What Is Remembered Lives* and *Walking in Beauty*.

AIR SHOWS UP in the tarot, bringing with it all of the positive healing qualities and all of the chaos that is part of this element. The minor arcana of the tarot is a reflection of the four elements, with the suit of swords being connected to the element of air. The energy of swords is related to communication, thinking, and the intellect. These cards are often connected to consciousness and thought. They can be a sign of a troubled mental state or a message that more clarity and thought are needed about a particular situation.

The suit of swords has gotten a bad reputation in the tarot reader world. People often think of swords as cards of trouble, difficulty, and conflict. Swords cards can suggest conflict, issues with power dynamics, or change. But more often than not, swords are a sign that you need better communication or clarity. It can also be a sign that you need to make some decisions. When many swords show up in a tarot reading, it can signify a need to be clear on a mental struggle, fear, or conflict. Swords may be a sign of challenges to come. Most often, swords will show you that it is time to be more aware of what is going on around you and not take anything at face value.

A sword has a double edge, and the cards of this suit reflect the balance of intellect and power. What can cure can kill—and what can hurt can also cut away what no longer serves. And because swords are also connected to communication, they also point to the power of words and how words can offer clarity, soothing, conflict, or pain. Air is an unseen force. It is in constant motion, but goes mostly unnoticed. It can be a destructive force or a cleansing breeze. Either way, the power of air is one of change—and this shows up in the relationship to swords in the tarot, both the total suit and beyond.

It's not only the cards from the suit of swords where we find the power of air in the tarot. The aces of every suit have the airy power of new beginnings, change, and spiritual matters. These powers are often represented on the cards as hands that emerge from a gust of wind to hold the sword, cup, pentacle, or wand in the air. The major arcana cards are also filled with air symbolism. Air is power, mental rules, and intellect, and these messages show up in several other cards:

The Fool: The beginning of the journey, the first step, the energy of the dawn. All of these powers are connected to the direction of east and therefore, the power of air.

The Magician: The symbolism of all of the suits is reflected in this card. The Magician is not the ruler of air, but rather capable of manipulating all of the elements.

The Emperor: The artwork of this card shows a masculine leader perched on a throne on the cliffside of the mountain. He is the ultimate ruler, using reason and thought as his guide. He is the ultimate symbol of the power of air.

Justice: The sword is seen again in the artwork of this card. It is pointed upward, held in one hand with the scales held in the other. This reflects the double-edged nature of the sword, along with rules and consequences.

Judgment: Air shows up in the artwork of this card as the horn being played by the angel Gabriel. It is a calling, music, awakening—all carried on the air. The sounds wake those that were slumbering and calls them to something more.

The World: Much like the Magician, the World holds mastery over all of the elements. The artwork of this card shows a person dancing on the world with the symbols of the four suits around them. They have achieved mastery, they know the mystery, and they are able to work alchemy with the four elements together.

A deeper understanding of air and how to work with it in our own lives can be gained by studying the messages of the cards.

Phoenix LeFae

• • • •

Work Your Magic

Think of all the correspondences in this chapter as ways to assist your understanding of the element of air. Once you know what the element of air feels like, you'll have a more intuitive understanding of how you consciously and unconsciously wield it. Let these qualities inspire you to a higher level of air magic. If you wish to create a strong association with the element of air, use these ideas and tools often.

Chapter 6

AIR HERBS AND BOTANICALS

The plant correspondences in this chapter are messengers of the element of air. They're energetic conduits between the elemental realm of air and the physical plane. They can be used to help you find the most precise energy for your air magic.

Air-corresponding plants often have a certain appearance—their branches and leaves are daintily splayed in the air. The plants' affinity for growing in this manner shows how much they're in harmony with the element of air. It's as if they want to reach out and embrace it.

This chapter provides the traditional meanings of air-corresponding plants. You'll also find some plants and meanings that are usually associated with other elements. For example, plants used for love magic are thought of as water correspondences, and herbs that promote good health usually are associated with the element of earth. The best way to think about these apparent elemental inconsistencies is that the plants in this list can create the proper mindset to allow those qualities to manifest. By enabling the right mentality, you invite the energy of the physical, emotional, and spiritual to take form. In other words, the element of air activates the other elemental qualities into being.

Some of these plants can be made into an herbal infusion or incense, but you don't need to burn or consume them to reap their benefits. Often, merely being in the presence of the plant and communing with its spirit is enough to gain insights. Try sitting with it and enjoying its presence. Exchange energy and have a light dialogue with it. Another way to work with plant energy is to carry a piece of it with you or place it somewhere where you want to see the effects. Of course, plants are also useful in charm bags or spell jars.

If you harvest plants in the wild, do so sustainably and with certainty about the identification so you don't touch or consume poisonous plants. Use reliable guidebooks to learn their proper identification and preparation. When harvesting, only take what you need. Be sure to leave the plant with a healthy amount of leaves and bark so it can continue to grow and supply other people and animals. Consult with a doctor or an herbalist before consuming any plants that aren't already commonly used in cooking or teas.

As you read through this list of air magic plants, imagine you're in the presence of the plant. If it has an aroma, take a deep breath and conjure the scent within your mind. Get it touch with it spiritually and feel what energies it evokes within you.

Plants

Plants are powerful allies for magical practitioners. The plants in this list all have air properties—some assist with communication or mental clarity. Others are protective and cleansing, which reflect air's ability to keep negativity away. Several of these plants promote change, while others have spiritual aspects.

Agrimony *(Agrimonia gryposepala* or *A. striata)*: This plant, with its tall stalks with golden flowers, is strongly protective. It's able to banish negativity and break curses. It's also good for spiritual healing. Some people have used it to detect the presence of Witches. To find like-minded friends, carry it in your pocket. It's associated with Mithras.

Anise *(Pimpinella anisum)*: Anise is a tall, airy plant with brown seeds that have a sweet, spicy aroma. It wards off nightmares, increases psychic and divination abilities, and assists in calling upon spirits. Anise can also be used for protection. It's linked to Apollo, Hermes, and Mercury.

Aster *(Aster novi-belgii)*: Asters were named after stars, and looking at their radiant petals, it's easy to see why. This plant easily elevates energy and promotes inner strength. Aster opens doorways and facilitates transitions, helping with fresh starts and new beginnings. It's also considered a protective plant—think of the blossoms as open eyes, ever watchful for negative energy. For this reason, many Witches plant it around their homes as a natural ward. Aster is associated with the Fae and Venus.

Bergamot, also known as bee balm *(Monarda didyma* or *M. fistulosa)*: Bergamot is a fragrant herb that aids in the success of all spells. It adds logic, peace, awareness, prosperity, luck, and good energy. It is associated with Gaia and Persephone.

Butcher's broom *(Ruscus asculeatus)*: The branches of this evergreen shrub were historically used to make small brooms. Sweep your magical space with one to energetically cleanse it and protect it. Butcher's broom can also be used in weather magic—tossing a branch into the air stirs the winds, and burning a branch makes the winds die down. It's sometimes burned to calm the nerves and to enhance visionary powers. This plant is connected to Amon, Ares, Jupiter, and Mars. Butcher's broom should not be confused with the poisonous broom shrub, which has yellow flowers.

Caraway *(Carum carvi)*: Caraway has aromatic, savory seeds that protect against negativity and theft. They stimulate health, love, libido, and fidelity. They also strengthen mental abilities and aid in memory retention. It is linked to Mercury.

Chicory *(Cicorium intybus)*: This plant, with its tall stalks and periwinkle flowers, can grow nearly anywhere. It has the magic of perseverance. It's also used for success, especially when the chances are against you, as it unlocks doors and removes obstacles. This plant is associated with Apollo.

Clover *(Trifolium pretense* or *T. repens)*: Clover is another plant that's found nearly everywhere. It usually has three leaves, but some naturally occurring genetic mutations can produce four-leaf clovers and a higher number of leaves on the same stem. Clovers with four or more leaves enable psychic powers and spirit work. The flowers of this plant promote internal cleansing and general good health. Magically, clover attracts wealth, money, success, strength, love, protection, luck, and social stature. It's a sacred plant to the Fae, and spending time with it can assist in communicating with them. Linked to Gwydion.

Comfrey, also known as knitbone *(Symphytum officianale)*: This squat plant, with its wide, hairy leaves and little purple flowers, is a powerhouse for healing. It's often used externally in salves and poultices to heal wounds. Comfrey leaves stimulate the repair of tissues and reduce the healing time of bruises and sprains. The healing ability of this plant was known by the ancient Greeks, who named it sympho, which means "unite." Likewise, the Celts called it knitbone.

Magically, comfrey heals the source of problems in order to correct them. Comfrey can be used in reconciliation magic, for healing relationships and mental problems, and to find peace of mind. It's also a great travel companion, providing protection and prosperity. Use this plant externally only, as it contains chemicals that may be poisonous if ingested. Associated with Hekate.

Daisy *(Bellis perenis* or *Chrysanthemum leucanthemum)*: With their sunny flower heads and white petals, daisies easily evoke feelings of innocence and happiness. They're reminders that life can be beautiful at times. Daisies brighten energy and act as catalysts, promoting connections. Their energy inspires relaxation, mental health, and simplicity. Daisies are often used in wealth magic and to attract love. Connected to Aphrodite, Artemis, the Fae, Freya, Thor, Venus, and Zeus.

Dandelion *(Taraxacum officinale)*: Dandelion is a sunny flowering plant that has the ability to grow anywhere. It's great for perseverance magic, and it can be used for resiliency in order to power ahead. Dandelions bring cheerfulness and assuage depression.

When this flower transforms into a cluster of fluffy seeds, it's used in magical work to assist with change, to have grace during transitions, and to adapt to new circumstances. Make a wish and blow the seeds as hard as you can to cause change and to bring success from far and wide. Dandelion root promotes protection, purification, balance, psychic abilities, and the ability to work with spirits. Sacred to Brigid and Hekate.

Elecampane *(Inula helenium)*: This tall plant with yellow flowers attracts love and is used for magical protection. When burned as incense, it promotes psychic powers, especially visual ones such as scrying. Sacred to the Fae and Mercury.

Eyebright *(genus Euphrasia)*: Eyebright is a small herb with multi-colored flowers. It's commonly used to treat eye infections and allergy symptoms. Tea made from the flowers clears the air passages and strengthens mental powers, memory, and visual psychic abilities. It also increases happiness, living up to its namesake after Euphrosyne, the goddess of joy and mirth.

Fennel *(Foeniculum vulgare)*: The flowers and seeds of this sweet herb soothe and uplift the spirit. It's often prepared in teas or chewed to promote digestive health, treat urinary disorders, relieve menstrual cramps, increase breast milk, and improve halitosis. Anglo-Saxons used it to ward off evil, and ancient Romans used it to increase courage, longevity, and strength. Use fennel magically for protection, luck, to raise spirits, and to connect with the upper chakras. Sacred to Adonis, Dionysus, Hephaestus, Odin, and Prometheus.

Fenugreek *(Trigonella foenum-graecum)*: This clover-like plant produces fragrant yellow seeds that are often used in money magic and to create abundance. The seeds can also be used in protection and healing. Associated with Apollo.

Fern *(Polypodium vulgare)*: These plants, with their frilly fronds, have survived eons without changing. The leaves are used for longevity, luck, protection, wealth, and good health. The smoke from burning fern leaves exorcises bad spirits. Connected with the Fae, Kamapuaʻa, and Mercury.

Forget-me-not *(Myosotis genus)*: The beautiful blue flowers of the forget-me-not plant have a gentle, uplifting energy. They help with all kinds of mental powers, including focusing, memory, and mental health. Forget-me-not aids in finding perspective and simplicity by aligning the mind, body, and spirit. It's also used in love magic and for success. Associated with Persephone and Zeus.

Goat's Rue *(Galega officinalis)*: Also known as French lilac. This herb has clusters of purple blossoms and is used to increase mental powers such as reason and logic. It promotes physical and emotional healing. Connected with Ea, Faunus, and Pan.

Goldenrod *(Solidago genus)*: Goldenrod was named after the tiny golden flowers that form on the end of its tall green stalks. It attracts money, luck, success, and love. It's also used for divination and acts as a magical accelerant. Its pollen is a common allergen that travels long distances on the wind—use it when you want your magic to spread far and wide. Connected with Hermes, Hestia, and Inti.

Gotu kola *(Centella asiatica)*: This herb has fan-shaped leaves and is related to parsley. It assists with mental focus and provides a clear mental path toward goals. It also stills the mind for meditation. Associated with Sekhmet and Shakti.

Hops *(Humulus lupulus)*: Hop bushes have beautiful green flower-cones that look like they would chime in the breeze. There are several varieties of hops, with fragrances that range between floral, bitter, sweet, and skunky. The flowers are often used in making beer and are also used in teas to treat nerves and bring sleep. Linked to the Fae and Odin.

Hyssop *(Hyssopus officinalis)*: This small mint-family shrub is associated with purification, binding, and protection. It also improves mental focus. Connected to Jupiter.

Lavender *(Lavendula officinalis* or *L. angustifolia)*: With its deep purple flowers standing on tall green stalks, lavender is a well-known beneficial herb famous for its powers of relaxation and spiritual restoration. One whiff of the flowers can purify, banish negativity, clear the mind, and soothe stress. Lavender uplifts the spirits and promotes a feeling of spiritual transcendence. It acts as a natural anti-depressant, giving greater confidence, self-esteem, and emotional strength. Lavender assists with love and fidelity by promoting communication. When burned as incense, it assists with divination. It's also used to induce sleep and aid in digestive and respiratory problems.

Lavender oil is commonly used in blessings and ceremonies to open initiates up to the gods and spirits. It connects people with their intuition and life purpose. The ancient Egyptians and Greeks used lavender often, and earlier cultures likely did as well. Energetically, it's associated with the crown chakra and the third eye. Associated with the Fae, Hekate, Saturn, and Vesta.

Lemongrass *(Cymbopogon citratus)*: This lemony-smelling grass is commonly used in food to add a unique flavor. It stimulates mental focus, psychic abilities, divination, and lust.

Marjoram *(Origanum majorana* or *O. vulgare)*: Marjoram is a herbaceous, warming, antiseptic herb that's similar to oregano, but it's much milder. Its leaves are used as a stimulant and an expectorant. Ancient Egyptians used it to calm fevers, nerves, and headaches, and to stimulate the digestion. The ancient Greeks made garlands from the plant and gave them to newlyweds as a blessing for fertility, love, and happiness. Marjoram is used for grounding, healing, social stature, protection, health, and compassion. Connected to Aphrodite and Venus.

Mastic *(Pistacia lentiscus)*: Mastic is an evergreen shrub whose leaves and berries can draw the right things and people to you, especially if you're looking for love or friends. Burn its resin as incense for psychic abilities and to connect with spirits. Associated with Mercury.

Mint *(genus Mentha)*: There are over two thousand varieties of mint, including peppermint, spearmint, chocolate mint, water mint, and pineapple mint. It's a perennial herb common to many gardens. It usually has straight stems and dark green leaves that form opposite one another.

Mint's magic is all about transforming the present situation into something better. It repels negativity, soothes nerves, and assists with healing and health. It also combats depression, stress, and anger. Tea made from the plant treats digestive problems and relieves fever symptoms. Mint clears away headaches and increases mental focus. It's a great herb for prosperity, purification, social stature, love, fertility, wealth, travel, and success magic. Certain varieties, including peppermint, induce psychic abilities. Associated with Pluto, Venus, and Zeus.

Mistletoe *(Viscum album* or *Phoradendron flavescens)*: Mistletoe is a poisonous, evergreen shrub with red or white berries. It's a parasitic plant, and it draws life from whatever tree it grows upon. Because it's not entirely of the earth or air, it's thought of as a liminal plant, existing between states. It's traditionally used to clear the negative energy of the old year and welcome in the new year. Mistletoe is used in magic for fertility, hunting, protection, and love. A kiss beneath the mistletoe is supposed to guarantee eternal love. This plant also increases positive communication, good dreams, and confidence. Connected with Arianrhod, Asclepius, Balder, the Fae, Freya, Jupiter, Loki, Odin, Venus, and Zeus.

Mugwort *(Artemisia vulgaris* or *A. argenteum)*: This bitter herb with toothed leaves and tiny white blossoms is found nearly all over the world. Mugwort is a deeply spiritual plant. It opens the third eye and encourages astral projection, intuition, prophecy, lucid dreams, and visions. It has been brewed in beer since at least medieval times, and sailors smoked it as a mild hallucinogen to make the long voyages more interesting. Mugwort repels evil spirits and facilitates communication with spirit guides. Other magical uses of mugwort include wisdom, strength, health, healing, and creativity. When it's burned as incense, the aromas are useful for divination. Sacred to Artemis, Diana, Hekate, and Odin.

Nutmeg *(Myristica fragrans)*: It's theorized that Nostradamus used nutmeg, amongst other herbs, for divination and psychic abilities. Originating from tropical islands in Southeast Asia, nutmeg's spicy, warm aroma is often found in baked goods like pumpkin pie and chai spice cookies. It calms nerves and relieves insomnia and digestive problems. Nutmeg is a lucky herb, and it boosts happiness and banishes negativity. It gives greater confidence, concentration, a fresh start, wealth, art, and power. A slight hallucinogen, it also has a spiritual aspect, promoting astral projection, greater connection with intuition, lucid dreams, visions, and divination. Mace, a spice made from the covering of nutmeg seeds, can be burned as an incense to increase psychic abilities and sharpen the mind. Avoid ingesting large doses of nutmeg and mace, which could be toxic. Sacred to Munsin and Oyá.

Parsley *(Petroselinum crispum)*: Parsley is a green, leafy herb found all over Europe and the Americas. The ancient Greeks wove it into garlands to adorn winning athletes, and the ancient Romans wore a sprig of it to protect them against death, but the herb is also associated with death and funeral rites. It's an all-around health-boosting herb. Magically, it's used for power, wealth, passion, social stature, strength, divination, purification, and cleansing. It was associated with the Greek hero Archemorus, who was said to outrun even death. When he eventually died, parsley sprang up where his blood fell. Sacred to Persephone.

Rosemary *(Rosemarinus officinalis)*: This fragrant, clean-smelling shrub with purple flowers assists with memory and intellect. It's thought to be one of the first plants to be used for incense. The ancient Romans commonly burned it in their temples as well. Rosemary is associated with the Fae, Hestia, Rhiannon, and Zeus.

Sage *(Salvia officinalis* or *S. lavandulifolia)*: This herbaceous plant from the mint family provides access to mental clarity and wisdom. Sage amplifies the inner voice and intuition. It uplifts, cleanses, and activates both higher and lower chakras, creating serenity and a grounded enlightenment. Sage can be used in money magic and to remove energetic blocks. It's often burned for divinatory purposes and to provide protection, especially from spirits. It's associated with ancestor spirits, Athena, Gaia, Rhiannon, and Jupiter.

Starflower, also known as borage *(Borago officinalis)*: Starflower is named after its beautiful clusters of drooping blue flowers. The ancient Greeks made wine with it, and it's thought to be the secret ingredient in "the wine of forgetfulness" mentioned in *The Odyssey*. Borage is derived from the Celtic word *borrach*, meaning courage. Before leaving for battle, medieval villagers gave knights borage flowers for that purpose. Use starflower to calm nerves, aid in psychic awareness, to create a stronger will, and for protection. Associated with the muse Calliope.

Summer Savory *(Satureja hortensis)*: This fragrant green herb with fine stems and delicate leaves assists with mental abilities by strengthening focus and facilitating insight. Connected to Bacchus, Pan, and Mercury.

Thyme *(Thymus vulgaris* or *T. serpyllum)*: This diminutive shrub has tiny, fragrant leaves that repel insects and have anti-fungal and anti-bacterial properties. It promotes health and relieves cold symptoms. Magically, thyme acts in a similar manner—it cleanses the mind by destroying unwanted thoughts and feelings. Thyme helps you be your true self and find your soul's calling. It also has psychic properties and increases intuition. When burned as incense, it purifies and cleanses a space, aids in divination, and promotes communication with spirit guides and the Fae. It's also sacred to Hestia and Odin.

Wormwood *(Artemisia absinthium)*: This plant, with its tall, silvery fronds, is the primary flavoring for absinthe. Wormwood increases clairvoyance and psychic abilities, brings about change, and increases one's power. It's also used in love magic and is commonly burned for good luck. It's toxic in large doses. Associated with Artemis, Chiron, Diana, the Fae, Hekate, and Iris.

Vervain, also known as verbena *(Verbena officinalis)*: Vervain has clusters of tiny purple flowers and is known as the enchanter's herb. Like mint, there are several varieties, the most common of which is lemon verbena. Druids wore crowns made of the herb for magical protection during rituals. Roman priests and priestesses made brooms with it and swept their temples and altars with them. Vervain is often prepared as a tea to relieve headaches and promote relaxation. It repels insects, aids in digestion, and treats depression.

Magically, it's a good all-around plant. It uplifts emotions and raises energetic vibrations. It increases intuition, luck, inspiration, artistic ability, wealth, learning, abundance, love, fertility, peace, protection, healing, and inner strength. It can also be used in divination and attracting spirits. Vervain is sacred to the Fae—if you add vervain tea to your bath, you'll dream of them. Associated with Cerridwen, Demeter, Diana, Epona, Hermes, Isis, Jupiter, Juno, Mars, Mercury, Persephone, Thor, and Venus.

Yarrow *(Achilleamille folium)*: This member of the aster family produces tall clusters of small white flowers. Yarrow is a protective herb that relieves depressive feelings by causing an energetic shift toward a peaceful, higher vibration. It's used in love magic, shapeshifting, divining a soul's path, and precognition.

Its blossoms can heal wounds and are even said to stanch bleeding. Burn yarrow as incense to induce a trance. Connected with Cernunnos and the Fae.

Trees

Many pagan religions have a belief that trees are ancient spirits with great wisdom and power. Consider using a wand made from one of the trees in this section if you value intellect, communication, learning, and spirit work above other magical purposes. Nearly every part of a tree can be used in magical works or for incense, including the leaves, flowers, berries, seeds, wood, and bark (except for trees that are poisonous, of course).

If you want to harvest anything from a tree for use in your magic, always do so with reverence to the spirit of the tree. It's wise to follow the common folklore of asking the tree three times and receiving a positive answer each time to ensure you have the tree's permission. Consider giving the tree a gift of water in exchange.

Acacia *(Acacia arabica)*: The acacia tree is native to tropical areas, and the aromatic wood from the acacia tree is often used in sacred fires. It's highly protective and is useful for magic involving money and friendship. The sap, known as gum arabic, makes a sweet, fragrant incense that's used for cleansing, psychic work, and spirituality. This tree is sacred to Astarte, Diana, Ishtar, Krishna, Osiris, and Ra.

Apple *(Malus domestica)*: This tree is often called the tree of the afterlife and the otherworld. It's also associated with challenges, creativity, success, wealth, power, magic, and divination. Linked with Aphrodite, Apollo, Badb, Cailleach, Diana, Eros, the Fae,

Flora, Freya, Hera, Idunn, Lugh, Mabon, Macha, Manannan, Pomona, Rhiannon, Venus, Vertumnus, and Zeus.

Aspen *(Populus tremuloides)*: Aspen is a type of poplar with white bark and heart-shaped leaves. It helps with communication, especially about emotions. It increases sensitivity and connection with intuition. Aspen also protects and is associated with the underworld. This tree is connected with Apollo, Danu, Frigg, Gaia, Hekate, Hermes, the Morrigan, Odin, Persephone, and Zeus.

Banyan fig *(Ficus benghalensis)*: The banyan fig is a beautiful, sprawling tree also known as the Bodhi tree. It's associated with awakening, enlightenment, magic, learning, wisdom, the underworld, death, and spirituality. Linked with Brahma, Krishna, Shiva, Vishnu, and Yama.

Bay laurel *(Laurus nobilis)*: Bay laurel is an evergreen shrub or tree that assists with psychic work including divination, visions, clairvoyance, dream work, prophecy, and omens. It banishes negativity and gives clarity, peace, and power. Also associated with the Fae and weather magic. Its leaves are often burned as an offering. The deities associated with the bay laurel are Adonis, Apollo, Artemis, Asclepius, Balder, Ceres, Cernunnos, Dionysus, Fides, Gaia, Helios, Krishna, Mars, and Ra.

Benzoin *(Styax benzoin)*: This tall Indonesian tree has delicate white flowers. The resin from this tree is commonly burned as incense that has a sweet, almost vanilla-like aroma. Benzoin smoke removes stagnant energy and purifies a space. It's also used in prosperity magic.

Cedar *(Cedrus libani* or *Cedrus atlantica)*: This aromatic, ever-green giant clears away negativity with ease and increases luck, especially when burned as incense. Magically, it promotes strength, peace, divination, and spirit work. Cedar is linked to the deities Aegie, Arianrhod, Artemis, Astarte, Baal, Brigid, Ea, Enki, Odin, Osiris, Persephone, and Ra.

Crabapple *(genus Malus)*: The white and pink blossoms of this tree heal the mind from repetitive thoughts and depression. Crabapple flowers gently remove external expectations and promote self-acceptance, self-love, and self-worth. They also instill a greater appreciation of life. Associated with Odin, Nimue, and the deities linked to the apple tree.

Elder *(Sambucus canadensis)*: Also known as Witchwood, the Witch's Tree, and the Fairy Tree. The elder tree or shrub is a showstopper nearly all year round, with characteristics of the maiden, mother, and crone. Every spring, it produces beautiful clusters of white flowers that almost outnumber the leaves.

Magically, elder trees are used for protection, compassion, growth, prosperity, healing, fidelity, social stature, wealth, peace, communication, and wisdom. They can also increase psychic ability, spirituality, and the ability to divine. Sacred to Berchta, Boann, Cailleach, the Dagda, Danu, the Fae, Freya, Freyr, Gaia, Hel, Holle, Rhea, Venus, and Vulcan.

Eucalyptus *(Eucalyptus obliqua)*: Eucalyptus is an Australian native with a woody stem and leaves that have a menthol aroma. It opens the sinuses, treats symptoms of sickness, and repels insects. Magically, the leaves are used for purification, protection, health, and healing. Associated with Mercury.

Fir *(Abies amablis, A. balsamea, or A. concolor)*: This tall evergreen is associated with divination, spiritual growth, the otherworlds, transformation, protection, and spirits. It can increase mental powers such as memory, wit, insight, and learning. Its resin is often harvested from its pinecones for incense. Connected with Adonis, Artemis, Athena, Bacchus, Boruta, Cybele, Diana, Dziwitza, Frigg, Idunn, Inanna, Isis, Osiris, Pan, Persephone, and Rhea.

Ginkgo *(Gingko biloba)*: This distinctive tree, with its fan-shaped leaves, is thought to be the oldest tree on earth, as it has remained unchanged for the last 200 million years. Ginkgo leaves increase mental focus and intelligence. They also facilitate communication with the spirit world. It's associated with divinity and spirit in all of its myriad forms and is especially useful when doing animistic magic.

Hawthorn *(Crategus monogyna or C. douglasii)*: Hawthorn is also known as the May Tree due to its spectacular flowers that burst into bloom all over the tree around May. It also produces clusters of red berries. It's associated with family, love, fertility, and the cycles of life. It assists in creativity, happiness, love, rebirth, and purification. Hawthorn also protects against baneful magic. Linked to Belenus, Brigid, Cardea, the Dagda, Danu, the Fae, Frigg, Hera, Olwen, Prometheus, Thor, and Zeus.

Hazel *(Corylus avellana or C. americana)*: Hazel trees and shrubs are identifiable by their hardy, alternate, toothed leaves and smooth, light brown bark. It's associated with wisdom, luck, love, beauty, intuition, creativity, fertility, and the ability to summon and attract. Eating hazelnuts increases one's magical powers, especially divination and clairvoyance. This tree is sacred to Aphrodite, Arianrhod, Artemis, Boann, Danu, Diana, the Fae, Mabon, Manannan, Mercury, Ogma, Silvanus, Thor, and Venus.

Holly *(Ilex aquifolium, I. opaca,* or *I. verticillata)*: The holly family has trees, bushes, and climbers with dark green, prickly leaves and red berries. Holly promotes sacred space, opens the crown chakra, and provides a connection with the world of the gods and spirits. It releases mental blocks and clarifies the mind. It also provides protection from harm, be it physical, emotional, mental, or supernatural. Use caution with holly berries, as they're mildly poisonous. Associated with Ares, Cailleach, Cernunnos, the Dagda, Danu, the Fae, Faunus, Freyr, Gaia, the Green Man, Hel, Holle, Lugh, and Saturn.

Lilac *(Syringa vulgaris* or *S. baibelle)*: This bushy tree produces giant clusters of purple, blue, and white flowers with intoxicating floral aromas. Lilac assists with all kinds mental processing, including the power of imagination, receiving information, and creativity. It's used for harmony, divination, and to assist in shapeshifting. Connected to the Fae, Pan, and the nymph Syringa.

Linden *(Tilia eruopaea, T. americana, T. glabra,* or *T. canadensis)*: This giant deciduous tree has an asymmetrical leaf, delicate white flowers, and small hanging fruits that form out of a pale leaf-like projection. Linden increases all magic, and it's often used in attraction, love magic, creativity, healing, peace, and luck. It's also used for divination, dream work, and visions. This tree is sacred to Arianrhod, the Fae, Freya, Frigg, Odin, Ostara, Phylira, and Venus.

Maple *(Acer campestre, A. saccharum,* or *A. rubrum)*: The maple tree has distinctive lobed leaves with five to seven points. It represents abundance, prosperity, balance, family, support, wisdom, and endless love. As such, maples are lovely additions to neighborhoods or anywhere you wish to foster positive community growth. Maple produces a sweet syrup that can be used in cooking and baking to increase family ties. Connected to Athena, Nanaboozho, Rhiannon, and Venus.

Myrrh *(Commiphora myrrha)*: The sap from this spiny shrub is used to create myrrh resin. When burned, it creates a dark, sweet aroma. Myrrh is used to bring energy into balance, to cleanse and purify, to increase success and abundance, in manifestation, for protection, and to increase psychic powers. It's associated with Adonis, Aphrodite, Bast, Cybele, Demeter, Hekate, Isis, Juno, Ra, Rhea, and Saturn.

Oak *(Quercus robur, Q. alba,* or *Q. velutina)*: This majestic tree has strong, sprawling limbs and raised roots. These features make the oak's association with the otherworld clear. The oak is revered by the Druids, and it's also deeply linked with the Fae. Magically, oak is used for power, blessings, healing, courage, longevity, protection, knowledge, inspiration, spirit work, energy work, fertility, strength, wisdom, and prophecy. Oak is also linked to many gods including Aegir, Artemis, Asherah, Balder, Brigid, Ceres, Cernunnos, Cerridwen, Cybele, the Dagda, Demeter, Dôn, Donar, Fortuna, the Green Man,

Hades, Helios, Hera, Janus, Jupiter, the Morrigan, Odin, Pan, Perun, Taara, Taranis, Thor, Rhea, and Zeus.

Olibanum *(Boswellia sacra)*: This short deciduous tree grows in the warm eastern regions of the world, and its sap is harvested as the resin frankincense. When burned, frankincense purifies and protects against negative energy, heals anxiety, increases awareness, and strengthens the power of any magic. It's also used in clairvoyance, divination, and spirit work such as astral projection and necromancy. This plant is sacred to Baal, Bast, Helios, Krishna, and Ra.

Sandalwood *(Santalum album)*: This graceful tropical tree has fragrant wood that smells sweet and slightly spicy. It's used as an incense to elevate and awaken the spirit while simultaneously calming the emotions. Sandalwood increases clairvoyance and divination, and it can be used for spirit communication as well. Currently, this tree is vulnerable to extinction, so it's wise to not use it much. Sandalwood is associated with Durga, Hathor, Kali, Oyá, Tara, and Venus.

Star Anise Tree *(Illicum verum)*: This evergreen tree forms star-like pods with aromatic brown seeds that are commonly used in baking. In magic, star anise gives the practitioner greater authority and power. Star anise increases divination abilities and sweetens any magic, bestowing positive energy and blessings. It's connected to Apollo, Mercury, Oyá, and Xi Shi.

Walnut *(Juglans nigra or J. cinera)*: These giant deciduous trees facilitate powerful psychic experiences, otherworld travel, and weather magic. Walnut also carries the energy of blessings, wealth, mental power, fertility, clarity, transformation, inspiration, and purification. This tree is sacred to Aphrodite, Apollo, Artemis, Astarte, Car, Carmenta, Carya, Diana, Dionysus, Jupiter, Rhea, Thor, Vishnu, and Zeus.

Witch Hazel *(Hamamelis virginiana* or *H. vernalis)*: This winter-blooming shrub with tiny yellow flowers promotes health and healing. Its name comes from the Middle English word *wych*, meaning flexible, a reference to its branches. Witch hazel bark tonic treats eyes and cleanses skin. Magically, it's a good herb for protection, love, divination, and creative inspiration. Associated with Hekate.

Yew *(Taxus canadensis* or *T. baccata)*: This evergreen has soft, short needles, acorn-like green fruits, and small, red, cup-shaped berries. It's known as the tree of the dead, and it's used for otherworld travel, psychic ability, visions, and communication with spirits. It also relates to the energy of change, strength, longevity, magic, and protection. It may be burned for divination, but it should never be consumed because all parts of the tree are poisonous. This tree is associated with Artemis, Astarte, Badb, Banba, Cailleach, the Dagda, Dione, Dôn, Hekate, Hel, Hermes, Holle, Loki, Lugh, Odin, Persephone, and Saturn.

Essential Oils

Essential oils are a great alternative to incense. They let you inhale the pure volatile oils of plants without the harmful effects of smoke. Just like incense, essential oils use the sense of smell, and they are very evocative. Although any essential oil could be used to call upon the element of air, the specific oils from the plants listed in this chapter are even more effective. Use them to increase your ability to harness air magic.

One of the best ways to use essential oils topically is to dilute them into a carrier oil and apply them to your body. Diluted essential oil makes a great massage oil and perfume. Pulse points like the wrists, neck, temples, and the back of the knees will warm the oil and encourage it to diffuse. Guidelines vary about diluting essential oils, with different sources saying anywhere from three drops to twenty-five drops of essential oil per ounce of carrier oil is appropriate. Look up the individual essential oil and be cautious in case an allergic reaction develops. If your concentration seems safe and you'd like a stronger smelling oil, increase the amount of essential oil a little at a time.

Another great way to use essential oils, especially for air magic purposes, is to create an essential oil mister in a spray bottle. Add ten to twenty-five drops of essential oil to two ounces of purified water, shake, and spray. If possible, use a glass bottle to avoid degradation of the plastic.

Yet another way to use essential oils is in a diffuser. Diffusers use fans, warmth, or vibration to volatilize the oils into the air. Essential oils can also be used on incense charcoal to create a strong burst of aroma.

Use caution when using essential oils, as they're extremely strong and may irritate the throat or lungs. Pets are more sensitive to this than we are. Look online to find out which oils don't agree with pets, and aromatize with caution.

Herbal Infusions/Teas

One particularly wonderful way to enjoy the plants associated with air is to brew them into a beverage. The magical properties of the edible herbs associated with the element of air commonly mirror their health benefits. For example, an herb that's magically good for communication, such as elderflower, often supports the throat and respiratory passages. An herb that's good for magically increasing positive thoughts, like mint, can be made into an herbal tea that boosts one's mental outlook. Making tea in and of itself is a magical act—for more about this, check out the tea spell in Chapter 11.

Drinking tea is one of the best ways to absorb the energy of the plant and increase your own power. Also, I don't know about you, but I love preparing a beverage and drinking it occasionally whenever I'm doing magical work. Whether tea is iced or hot, it always seems to support and enliven whatever I do. Other ways to use herbal tea infusions in your magic is to use them in spell bottles, aromatize them in the air, and use them in potions.

Your Air Garden

If you enjoy gardening, try growing your own plants, herbs, and trees. Observing the living plant's nature and energy can give you a greater understanding of it. If a garden isn't possible for you, imagine that you have a garden filled with the plants you regularly use. Hold them and visit them in meditation to learn from them.

To really enjoy working with these plants, combine them with other air correspondences in your magic. For example, to increase your intelligence, you could sip peppermint tea at dawn on an elevated floor of a university library while you study. To sharpen the power of the spoken word, hike to a hilltop while Mercury is in Gemini, burn a blue candle, hold an aspen leaf, and speak your truth into the wind. By combining these airy correspondences with your air magical practices, you can more easily align with the true nature of air and increase your chance of success.

Chapter 7

AIR CRYSTALS AND STONES

History reveals the rich connection between early humans and gemstones. Quartz crystals have been found at burial sites dating back to 75,000 BCE. Likewise, amethyst decorations have been found that date back to 25,000 BCE, and lapis lazuli and quartz were first crafted into jewelry in the seventh millennium BCE. These actions took place when the prevalent human mindset was animism—early humans associated those stones with unique energies, intelligences, and a spirit. Today, our love of gemstones continues, with greater access to an abundance of types of crystals and minerals than ever before.

Certain gemstones, minerals, and metals are associated with the element of air. It may seem strange to correlate them with air because they're so dense; however, it makes sense if you consider that they carry a frequency that resonates within the magical element of air. The rocks and metals in this chapter can be used in your magical practice to help you focus, communicate, and expand your consciousness. Many of the stones and metals in this chapter activate the throat chakra or the third eye chakra. Others elevate one's energy to the magical frequency of air.

One of my favorite ways to work with these materials is to align my energy with their internal structure. I hold a crystal or a piece of metal and imagine that I can see the internal structure of one of their molecules. Every crystalline and metallic object on earth is made of millions of tiny molecules that are stacked on top of each other to form a lattice, which forms the larger piece. With your mind's eye, imagine seeing this three-dimensional structure. It may appear to be square, rectangular, pyramidal, rhomboidal, or another geometric shape. The molecular structure of the crystal is important because it defines its vibration. Allow your personal energy to shift to follow the same vibratory pattern as the object. Let it affect your posture and breathing. If you're working with a crystal that has a point, such as a naturally created quartz crystal, you have the added benefit of being able to elongate your vibration with the point. An interesting variation of this is to envision yourself inside of the crystalline lattice, as a sort of meditation cave.

Another way to work with these materials is to put your energy into them to program them to reverberate with your desire. Do this by concentrating on your desire and holding the stone. Imagine your energy going into it until it is saturated with it. The stone will act as a beacon to spread that energy. Recharge it with your intention when it feels as if the energy is not transmitting your message as effectively as you wish.

Yet another way to work with stones is to hold one and feel what part of your body it stimulates. The stone will naturally boost the energy of that place and correct any imbalances. Simply holding a crystal in meditation or carrying one will affect you. Keep the stone close to your body when possible—wear them as jewelry or slip them into your pockets to carry the energy with you.

Air Minerals, Rocks, Crystals, and Stones

Amethyst: This violet form of quartz purifies and protects, especially with matters concerning the mind. Its name comes from the Greek word *amethystos*, which means "not intoxicated." It promotes clear thinking, logic, and good judgment. It also clears away headaches and improves memory and intelligence. Amethyst is a good meditation stone, promoting psychic abilities as well as a more spiritual life. It's known as a royal stone, and it was featured in many medieval crowns. Amethyst also corresponds with water due to its emotion-stabilizing qualities. It's associated with the zodiac sign Aquarius, the planet Neptune, and the deities Bacchus, Diana, Dionysus, Justitia, and Venus.

Apophyllite: This uplifting clear crystal may appear to be quartz at first glance, but it has a different structure and energy. It naturally uplifts, expands, and empowers the mind. It promotes crystal-clear thinking by organizing thoughts and information, giving fresh ideas and insights. Apophyllite stimulates all aspects of the mind and the third eye chakra.

Aventurine: This lovely dark green quartz has sparkling inclusions of mica. It stimulates the mind, increasing intelligence, analytical powers, and creativity. Considered an all-around lucky stone, it also promotes wealth and healing, especially for the heart. Aventurine is one of the birthstones of Cancer and Libra.

Charoite: Charoite is a deep lilac or violet stone with milky swirls. This gentle stone dissolves mental obstacles like fear and self-imposed limitations. It empowers soul-aligned vision and thought, and aligns one with their true path.

Danburite: This clear crystal might look like quartz at first glance, but it has a different crystal lattice. It carries a high vibration, activates mental and spiritual abilities, and opens the uppermost chakras. It can also connect people with spirits.

Fluorite: This stone has a wide range of colors, including violet, green, and clear. It forms tiny tetrahedron crystals. Fluorite stimulates the mind by increasing order and clarifying thoughts. It amplifies the ability of other stones around it, so it's a good stone to use in grids. Fluorite corresponds with the planet Neptune.

Herkimer Diamond: The double-terminated quartz crystal is an excellent stone to uplift thoughts and clarify the aura. It assists in developing awareness and sparking psychic powers, specifically clairvoyance and clairaudience.

Lapis Lazuli: Lapis is a gorgeous deep blue stone with flecks of gold-colored pyrite. It can be composed of several different minerals, which makes each piece unique. This stone assists with psychic abilities and communication with spirits and the gods. Lapis encourages a clear mind by loosening recumbent thoughts and allowing the mind to focus better. It clears away headaches and improves mood. Connected with Taurus and the planet Jupiter.

Lepidolite: This sparkly purple stone contains several facets of mica. It gently brings about psychic abilities and promotes a clear mind. Lepidolite also aids in spiritual endeavors, balance, peace, and luck.

Mica: Mica minerals can be found on their own or in many other stones. The larger pieces look like silvery sheets that can be flaked off with a fingernail. Smaller crystals are often embedded in other stones, which increase their sparkle or shine. Mica facilitates divination and psychic abilities. It also reveals the truth of a situation.

Moldavite: This glassy green stone was created when an asteroid struck the earth and cooled rapidly. It carries an extremely high vibration and opens the crown chakra. Moldavite is predominantly used for psychic and spiritual experiences, including astral projection, divination, and visions.

Opal (white): Called the "queen of gems" by Shakespeare, this light-colored mineral has flashes of opalescence that can include a rainbow of colors. Magically, opals encourage astral projection, protect the wearer, and magnify psychic power. They were revered by the Romans as a stone of hope and love. It's also known as the "stone of thieves" because of its rumored ability to make the wearer invisible. It correlates with Libra, Pisces, the planet Neptune, and the god Cupid.

Pumice: This gray stone looks like a sponge due to all its tiny holes. They're created when lava contacts air and cools quickly, creating stones with air pockets. Pumice stones are so light they actually float. Pumice assists in purifying energy and rising above negative emotions.

Quartz (clear): Clear quartz crystals are one of the most popular crystals because they're very adaptable to all kinds of magic. They're associated with the element of air due to their ability to open the mind and promote mental and spiritual awareness. Just holding one provides greater clarity, purification, and healing. They also activate psychic abilities, power, and visions. Associated with the Fae.

Quartz (smoky): Smoky quartz has the same shape as clear quartz, but it's a few shades darker due to the natural radiation of silicon when it formed. These lovely crystals can be gray, brown, black, translucent, or opaque. Smoky quartz is a powerful stone that has the same properties as clear quartz, and it also removes negativity from the aura. It assists in grounding negative energy and amplifying positive energy, which creates a safe energetic field for the wearer.

Selenite: This clear white mineral has an inner brilliance that makes it appear to glow from the inside out. It uplifts spiritual energy and is associated with the third eye and crown chakras. The ancient Greeks named it after Selene, the goddess of the moon. It's also associated with the goddess Luna.

Sodalite: Sodalite is a deep blue stone with streaks of white calcite. Wear it whenever you want to express yourself better. Sodalite empowers people to find vocal power and the right words. It's the perfect stone to wear when you're writing, creating music, or having a deep conversation. It's also good for meditation and healing the throat. Associated with Sagittarius.

Titanite, a.k.a. sphene: This rare, transparent titanium crystal has a wide range of colors, including red, orange, yellow, and green. It can increase the powers of the mind, analytical thinking, concentration, intelligence, and communication. Titanite is also associated with meditation and assists with spiritual endeavors.

Tourmalated quartz: The combination of clear quartz and shards of black tourmaline protects, grounds, and elevates energy into the spiritual realms. It also clears negativity away and promotes psychic abilities and astral projection.

Ulexite: This ultra-clear, naturally occurring crystal is sometimes called the vision stone or the television stone because it enhances the appearance of any flat object it's placed on. Ulexite does not project energy well, but it can be used to attune one's energy to the element of air.

Metals

Aluminum: This silver-colored, lightweight metal is flexible and adaptable. Because it's used in airplane parts and luggage, it's often used in travel magic. It's also linked with connecting, the mind, and power.

Tin: Tin is a lightweight, adaptable metal that's useful for all kinds of work. It looks like silver, but it's much lighter and more malleable. Tin increases luck, wealth, and the ability to divine the future. It's also connected to money and lust.

Cleansing and Charging Crystals and Stones

Cleanse your crystals and stones regularly to ensure they are clear of any other energy. One of the best ways to do this is with a cleansing breath. Focus on the element of air within you and take a deep breath. Blow on the stone and envision your breath removing any lingering energy on it.

Once a stone has been cleansed, it's a good idea to charge it. One of the most common ways to charge crystals is by moonlight or sunlight, so they absorb the energy of that celestial body, much like a solar panel. You can also charge crystals with your mind by focusing on a word or a feeling. Gaze at the stone and envision your thoughts programming it with this energy.

Carry a charged stone or crystal to sustain the energy and to keep it accessible for your everyday uses. Use them in magical work to make it more powerful.

Crystal Clear

Whenever you need a boost of air magic, stones and metals are a great resource. They can elevate the energy of your magic and help you bring forth your desired results. When they're not in use, store them on your air shrine or on your center altar to empower it with that energy.

Chapter 8

AIR ANIMAL GUIDES

Seeing a creature flying overhead is always a thrilling experience for me. Whether it's a vulture, a bat, a hummingbird, or a moth, there's a certain grace to their flights. They command the air around them, knowing that when they leap from a branch, they have the power to sweep the air beneath their wings and rise into the sky. Perhaps these flying creatures are so enthralling because humans can't fly without machines or equipment, or maybe it's because they evoke a light, uplifting feeling inside of our hearts. Whatever it is, I'm grateful to share the air with these masters of the aerial world.

Birds and Ornithomancy

Since ancient times, people have associated birds with different meanings. This kind of divination is called ornithomancy, and it's the largest category of augury. It was practiced by several ancient cultures, including the Mesopotamians, Egyptians, Greeks, Romans, and Celts. It was so popular in Rome and the Mayan Empire that each civilization had an entire college devoted to teaching priests how to interpret omens. These teachings focused heavily on the movement and cries of birds. Signs from birds were so important to the Romans that entire armies would wait to proceed until the birds gave a favorable sign.

Ornithomancy is interpreted as fate or the will of the gods. Many cultures thought omens from birds were better than omens from any other animal. Some believe it's because birds fly closer to the gods and spirits who reside in the air and the heavens. Another belief is that birds are the perfect vessels for omens because their natures are reactionary, like the wind. Other cultures associate birds with a spirit's flight at the moment of death. All of these concepts align with the qualities of air.

This section contains information about some of the more common birds, their traits, and their historical interpretations. If you wish to practice ornithomancy, ask for a sign and see what bird crosses your path. Generally speaking, an odd behavior is more significant than a normal one, such as seeing an owl during the daytime. Likewise, seeing a rare bird is a more important omen than seeing a common one. Birds seen flying to one's right were considered a sign of positive outcomes. Birds flying to the left meant delays and problems. If a bird flies toward you, it's a sign that good things will happen. Birds flying away from you mean that no opportunities will arise for this matter. Other good omens included birds flying high, birds singing while flying, and seeing a flock of birds. If no birds appear in your line of sight, the gods may not be interested enough to weigh in at the moment. Try again later or try another form of divination.

Traditional Meanings of Birds

- Albatrosses represent challenges, endings, travel, endurance, freedom, patience, transformation, a quest, spirituality, and strength.

- Blackbirds signify luck, courage, happiness, the home, the underworld, wisdom, rebirth, and spiritual work. Linked with Rhiannon.

- Bluebirds mean accomplishment, awakening, transformation, change, confidence, creativity, fertility, love, and motivation.

- Blue jays represent adaptability, assertiveness, courage, skillfulness, luck, magic, opportunities, and the underworld. Associated with the god Mars.

- Canaries represent fidelity, happiness, family and home, awakenings, beauty, friendship, healing, intuition, love, luck, and spirituality.

- Cardinals portray the home, family, happiness, balance, clarity, health, creativity, friendship, intuition, and love.

- Chickadees correspond with taking action, awakening, balance, cheer, truth, community, fertility, and mental powers.

- Chickens represent abundance, community, renewal, spirit work, and spirituality. Roosters' calls denote good luck, health, and protection from harm. They represent awakening, confidence, courage, solar energy, lust, and optimism. They're linked to Amaterasu, Apollo, Ares, Attis, Cerridwen, Helios, Hermes, Lugh, and Mercury.

- Condors are associated with taking action, healing, insight, leadership, boundaries, manifestation, protection, purification, rebirth, spirit work, and strength.

- Cranes represent abundance, transformation, focus, creativity, endurance, grace, balance, healing, justice, travel, intelligence, longevity, the astral realm, magic, logic, the underworld, patience, wisdom, peace, spiritual work, protection, independence, health, and rebirth/renewal. Also connected to Apollo, Artemis, Badb, the Fae, Hephaestus, Hera, Lugh, Manannan, and the Morrigan.

- Crows can be interpreted in several ways. Some cultures believed that seeing a crow or hearing its cry always brought disaster or evil with it. Other cultures believed that a cawing crow foretells of rain. Crows have also been known to reveal treachery. If you see one on your left, it's bad luck; if on your right, it's a caution to take care. Make a wish when you see a crow gliding. If it doesn't flap its wings, your wish may come true. Seeing two crows flying is considered good luck. Magically, crows relate to community, spirituality, protection, manifestation, destruction, the home, magic, intelligence, awareness, spiritual work, change, wisdom, creativity, intuition, rebirth, the afterlife, longevity, health, love, adaptability, motivation, and opportunities.

  A popular children's rhyme that counts crows or magpies goes, "*one for sorrow, two for joy, three for a girl, four for a boy, five for silver, six for gold, seven for a secret never to be told. Eight for a wish, nine for a kiss, ten for a bird you must not miss!*" This rhyme is thought to originate from a traditional poem: *"One for sorrow, two for mirth, three for a funeral, four for birth."*

Deities that correspond with crows include Amaterasu, Asclepius, Athena, Badb, Buddha, Cailleach, Hel, Macha, Maeve, Mithras, the Morrigan, Rhiannon, and Saturn.

- Cuckoos are thought to be bad luck by some cultures. This is likely due to the fact that they kill baby birds of other species and lay eggs in their nests. It's thought that if you hear a cuckoo call from the south or west, it's good luck. If from the east, it means love. If from the north, it's bad luck. The first time you hear a cuckoo cry in spring, check your belongings. If you have no money, it's a sign of very bad luck. Associated with adaptability, new beginnings, deceit, fate, justice, opportunity, spiritual work, and intuition. Also linked with Athena, Hera, Juno, and Pan.

- Doves are signs of peace, good luck, prosperity, fertility, love, wisdom, renewal, fidelity, healing, longevity, forgiveness, mental powers, grief, passion, and happiness. Associated with Aphrodite, Astarte, Demeter, Freya, Holle, Inanna, Ishtar, Isis, Maia, Rhea, and Venus.

- Ducks represent luck, abundance, transformation, affection, peace, emotional clarity, community, fidelity, opportunities, protection, and spiritual work.

- Eagles were thought by the Romans to be a sign of prosperity and good luck. If several eagles appear, their flight patterns may be observed for strategy in whatever matter is inquired. Magically, they correspond with prosperity, war, clarity, respect, enlightenment, freedom, strength, intuition, justice, activation, shapeshifting, longevity, confidence, magic, wisdom, motivation, opportunities, authority, success, peace, truth, spirit work and spirituality, purification, courage, renewal, passion, and awareness. Eagles correspond with Agni, Ares, Belenus, Isis, Jupiter, Justitia, Lugh, Odin, Pan, and Zeus.

• Falcon sightings are good luck, especially if the divination is for financial or relationship matters. They represent magic, clarity, strength, healing, intelligence, loyalty, a quest, and authority. Connected to Freya, Frigg, Horus, Khensu, Nephthys, and Ra.

• Finches represent community, awakenings, wealth, change, fertility, happiness, balance, renewal, community, spirit work, and awareness.

• Flamingo sightings are tied to abundance, transformation, balance, community, and stability.

• Geese are a sign of abundance, taking action, community, travel and a safe return, a quest, cooperation, fertility, the home, spirit work and spirituality, freedom, happiness, love, motivation, the underworld, and fidelity. Linked with Amun, Aphrodite, Bertha, Brahma, Geb, Hera, Isis, Juno, Odin, Osiris, and Ra.

• Hawks represent good luck and success, especially if they appear on your right side. However, witnessing a hawk capturing prey means you'll suffer a loss. Magically, they also correlate with the afterlife, the astral realm, authority, skillfulness, awareness, war, clairvoyance, truth, clarity, wisdom, courage, power, leadership, opportunities, and creativity. They're connected with Cerridwen, the Dagda, Danu, Hera, Hermes, Isis, Mercury, Nephthys, and Ra.

- Herons are associated with luck, abundance, spiritual work, the afterlife, protection against aggression, assertiveness, the astral realm, transformation, authority, wisdom, balance, hope, skillfulness, intelligence, magic, logic, and opportunities. They correspond with the Fae and the god Amun.

- Hummingbirds represent luck, balance, poise, strength, beauty, protection, endurance, forgiveness, happiness, travel, the Fae, healing, the home, spirit work, independence, health, intelligence, love, motivation, optimism, and purity.

- Kingfishers are good luck, especially for sailors. Seeing one at its nest means the weather will be calm and fair. They are associated with wealth, abundance, happiness, harmony, love, fidelity, and peace.

- Loons represent mysticism, the astral realm, independence, peace, romance, and dreams.

- Magpies are thought to be bad luck in many cultures. Their chatter means either a stranger will come to visit or some misfortune will visit the family. They also correlate with wealth, health, adaptability, change, skillfulness, intelligence, luck, manifestation, spirit work and spirituality, and opportunities.

- Nightingales represent beauty, healing, and hope.

- Owls represent wisdom, the underworld, sharp-sight, the unfathomable, nocturnal, and the mysterious. Many cultures associated seeing them with a warning of death. Some believed an owl's call was an omen of a terrible calamity or misfortune. They were considered by the Romans to be harbingers of death and bad luck. To the Greeks, they were a sign of good fortune. Also associated with the afterlife, mental powers, clairaudience and clairvoyance, truth, awareness, protection, dreams, spirit work, assertiveness, enlightenment, insight, intuition, shapeshifting, intelligence, magic, protection, the moon, the underworld, purification, rebirth, clarity, the astral realm, and opportunities. Owls are sacred to Ares, Artemis, Asclepius, Athena, Cailleach, Hekate, Indra, Lakshmi, and Minerva.

- Parrot sightings are associated with community, creativity, healing, and longevity.

- Peacocks represent attraction, pride, beauty, confidence, wisdom, longevity, manifestation, honesty, peace, wealth, abundance, protection, and renewal. They're linked to Amun, Brahma, Devi, Hera, Hermes, Hestia, Horus, Iris, Juno, Pan, Sarasvati, and Zeus.

- Pelicans are associated with challenges, kindness, magic, renewal, and grief.

- Pheasants relate to the energy of attraction, self-awareness, and confidence. Associated with Amaterasu.

- Pigeons represent family, the home, innocence, love, fertility, loyalty, peace, and luck.

- Ravens are clever birds, and they're a sacred bird of the augurs. Their appearance could indicate either a positive or negative outcome. They correlate with shapeshifting, affection, wisdom, courage, fate, healing, intelligence, clairvoyance, grief, magic, clarity, manifestation, change, rebirth, quests, mental powers, opportunities, the underworld, and protection.

  Many deities are associated with ravens, including Amaterasu, Apollo, Asclepius, Athena, Babd, Cailleach, Danu, Freya, Inanna, Lugh, Macha, Maeve, Mars, Mithras, the Morrigan, Odin, Rhiannon, Saturn, and Tiamat.

- Robins are good luck. Whenever you see one, make a wish. If it flies upward, you'll have very good luck. Robins also signify change, happiness, wisdom, luck, and spirit work. The god Belanus is linked with robins.

- Seagulls are associated with transformation, the afterlife, clarity, freedom, travel, friendship, intelligence, abundance, magic, spirit work, opportunities, action, and purification. They are linked to Aphrodite, the Fae, and Njord.

- Sparrows represent the home and signify hope. Magically, they relate to desire, fertility, happiness, awakenings, love, fidelity, loyalty, assertiveness, and manifestation. They are sacred to Aphrodite and Venus.

- Storks bring luck, new beginnings, compassion, renewal and rebirth, protection, creativity, wealth, spirit work, devotion, fertility, longevity, luck, opportunities, and fidelity.

- Swallows are considered bad luck by some; however, they're also associated with beneficial house spirits. They represent community, fertility, healing, the home, manifestation, hope, protection, renewal, and love. They are connected with Aphrodite, Inanna, Isis, and Ra.

- Swans represent luck, awakenings, balance, transformation, beauty, travel, change, devotion, desire, fidelity, trust, intuition, longevity, grace, healing, manifestation, the underworld, a quest, innocence, love, spirit work, and spirituality. Swans correspond with Angus, Aphrodite, Apollo, Bertha, Brahma, Brigid, the Fae, Manannan, Nemesis, Njord, Sarasvati, Venus, and Zeus.

- Turkeys represent abundance, fertility, gratitude, growth, self-work, and renewal.

- Vultures are thought to foretell of death. In war, the length of their flight represented how many soldiers would die. They're considered good luck if signs indicate that the deaths will be on the other side. Vultures are associated with the goddess Nekhbet, protection of children and mothers, the afterlife, trust, cycles, patience, purification, transformation, rebirth, and shapeshifting. They're also linked to Apollo, Ares, Hathor, Isis, Maat, Mars, Nephthys, Tiamat, and Zeus.

- Woodpeckers represent luck, spiritual work, awakenings, weather magic, mental powers, assertiveness, fertility, magic, protection, truth, and purification. They are sacred to Ares, Buddha, Jupiter, Mars, Pan, Silvanus, and Zeus.

- Wrens stand for good luck and awakenings, spirit work, strength, adaptability, purification, confidence, endurance, mental powers, happiness, and assertiveness.

Bats

The only mammal capable of true flight is the bat. You may have seen them wheeling overhead at dusk, swooping this way and that to catch mosquitos and other flying insects. Perhaps you've seen them visiting fruit trees at night to feed. There's a wide variety of bats. Different strengths and abilities are associated with each species. Bats are nocturnal, and they live all over the world, with the exception of extremely cold places. Many species pollinate plants and disperse seeds, which enables new life to occur.

In my undergraduate studies, a university in Brazil offered me an internship and the chance to research bats in the rainforests. I leaped at the chance to get closer to these mysterious, primal creatures of the night. Most of my work meant walking through the rainforest at night with thick gloves, a headlamp, and nearly invisible mist nets. We caught all kinds of bats, including a vampire bat. Holding these amazing creatures as they were measured was a phenomenal experience, and it cemented my adoration for them even more.

Magic associated with bats includes community, the subconscious, death, release of old habits, strength, endurance, longevity, new beginnings, magic, the underworld, rebirth and renewal, luck, change, spiritual work, wealth, transformation, and agriculture. They're also connected with Artemis, Diana, and Persephone.

Magical workings with bats should always be performed at night. Look for them in the skies starting around sundown. Check the internet for information about the kind of bats that live near you. If you're interested in a certain kind of bat, such as the giant flying fox, you may have to visit a zoo or a location where they're known to live. Draw local bats to you by hanging a bat house on a tree that gets a lot of sunshine.

Insects

Insects that fly are naturally associated with the element of air. With their unique beauty and graceful flight, they have inspired artists and poets for centuries. Insects that make noise, such as crickets, also correspond with the element of air due to the music they make.

- Bees are messengers between flowers, communicating pollen and initiating new life. They're essential for the fruit and vegetables for this year's harvest, and by extension of seeds, next year's harvest as well. With their hive mind and dancing form of communication, bee energy translates well to magic for community, working hard, and spreading new ideas. They're also associated with the underworld, abundance, wisdom, agriculture, focus, dreams, warrior energy, family, mental powers, motivation, and renewal. Bees have long been associated with Apollo, Cybele, Demeter, Diana, Iris, Krishna, Ra, and Vishnu.

- Butterflies often represent life after death because they undergo a metamorphosis as they transform from a caterpillar into a winged beauty. Several people believe butterflies carry messages from the deceased to us, especially during funerals and periods of grief. It was also said that Witches could transform into them. These pollinators are associated with beauty, freedom, rebirth, transformation, the Fae, dreams, travel, endurance, confidence, grace, trust, happiness, inspiration, love, magic, fidelity, agriculture, opportunities, manifestation, purification, fertility, spirit work, and the cycles of life.

- Cicadas, the long-resting insect, correspond with transformation, happiness, the home, success, honesty, longevity, and patience.

- Crickets are insects that fill the summer night air with their music. Their susurrus add to the warmth of the season and insulate against other noises, making the night feel cozy. Crickets are associated with messages or omens, cheerfulness, trust, endings, the home, intuition, luck, renewal, and protection.

- Dragonflies are among the fastest insects. They dart with the grace of a hummingbird, and they have a voracious appetite for mosquitos. They're associated with introspection, dream work, emotional support, self-preservation, the Fae, enlightenment, messages or omens, change, transformation, clarity, truth, boundaries, longevity, and passion. Sacred to Agni.

- Fireflies light up the night, shining a light on our darkness. They correspond with hope, accomplishment, inspiration, activation, enlightenment, and creativity.

- Moths are pollinators who represent moon magic, abundance, transformation, taking action, protection, mystical love, awakenings, and rebirth. Connected with Artemis and Hekate.

Sacred Feathers

If you want to connect with the natural element of air during your magical rites, try using a feather. Feathers have the benefit of having been used for flight, possibly for several years. This means they contain energies of air, flight, and the bird it came from. If possible, use a certain kind of feather that's appropriate for your magic. For example, an eagle feather would be ideal for someone whose magical workings are about gaining wisdom, justice, and peace.

Another use for feathers is to direct smoke over a person or object in order to cleanse them. Some people from Native American and Caribbean tribes use feathers or bird wings to waft smoke. Feathers were made to move air, so they direct smoke quite effectively.

There are a few cautions about working with feathers. Feathers can carry diseases such as salmonella. Use caution when touching them so as to not transmit any diseases. It's also advisable to not purchase a feather unless you know that it was sustainably collected. Never use plucked feathers, as this creates a traumatic association with the animal—use ones that have fallen naturally instead. Repurposing feathers or a wing from a deceased bird, such as one hit by a car, may be a sacred way to honor them and work with their spirit. If you desire a certain kind of feather, ask around—an avian center may have feathers for sale, or you may know a naturalist or a hiker who finds them regularly. However, be aware that it's illegal to own the feathers of certain species of birds because of the dangers of poaching, especially for threatened or endangered species.

Working With Animal Guides

If you're interested in working with one of these air creatures in particular, their energy may have much to teach you. Read books and watch videos about them. Look for them in the wild. When you find them, study their behavior and listen to what they seem to say to you. Think about how their traits can be activated within you.

If possible, feed them or give them a place to stay. With butterflies, this could mean planting the flowers they like. For birds, put out seed or cracked corn, and for bats, hang up a bat home. These creatures may also like fresh water too, and a bird bath could attract all kinds of birds to you. By inviting these animals into your life, you'll increase your association with them and your energetic exchange. This will also help you call upon them in magical workings.

Once you've established a rapport with the animal, call upon the energy of the creature in your magical works. If you wish, you can send some of yours into the skies as well. Any magical workings with birds should be associated with the time of the day when they're most active. For this reason, you might want to have connections with animals that are active during both the daytime and nighttime. If your connection with the animal is strong, use artwork or a photo of them on your air shrine or main altar. Seeing it will remind you of your deep connection with their energy, and it will inspire you to connect with them.

Your association with this animal may be a temporary learning experience, or it may be lifelong. Learn what you can from them while the connection is strong. When you no longer feel a strong affinity for the animal, you may have outgrown them. Do your research again and find another one that empowers you.

CHAPTER 8

Meeting a Bird Spirit

There are several bird sanctuaries, zoos, and bird rehabilitation centers where you can observe birds close up. Visiting one of these places is a great way to commune with the unique animalistic element of air. If you're not sure which bird you relate with most, this is an especially revelatory experience. When you're face to face with one, it's likely you'll get a concrete idea of their energy and whether you feel a connection or not.

Plan to leave your pets at home so the birds will be at ease. Also plan on not wearing strong or artificial fragrances, which can be disorienting to them. If you're interested in getting really close to one, call ahead to find out if the naturalists take the birds out of their cages.

When you visit the sanctuary or zoo, approach slowly and quietly. Give the birds plenty of space. Use diminutive body language, at least at first, to indicate you're not a threat to them. Observe the birds' body language and how they present themselves. Notice how they observe the world around them. Using your psychic abilities, sense their energy and their natural powers. For example, if you were visiting an eagle, you might notice its sharp, piercing eyes, its alertness, and its strength. If you were visiting a crow, you may see how playful it is or sense the way it thinks. Pay attention to how the bird interacts with you. Does it seem intrigued by your presence? Does it have a royal air about it?

If you're fascinated by one bird in particular, stay near them for a while. Without words, ask if it would like to exchange energy with you. If you sense a yes, send them love and receive a little back. If you feel a deep connection, plan a return trip to see the bird again. Consider making a donation to the organization or volunteering there. A monetary donation provides food and shelter. It also ensures the bird will be cared for, which is a true form of energy exchange.

Traditional Roman Ornithomancy

Many people practice a form of casual ornithomancy. They ask a question and interpret the birds that cross their path. Some people don't even ask a question—they just watch for whatever appears. There's nothing wrong with this, but there's always value to learning a traditional method, especially one that was refined for centuries, such as the Roman method.

Before you begin, decide how much time you will take to receive the message—it may be as little as fifteen minutes or as much as several hours. The amount of time should reflect the severity of the question. If you feel uncomfortable calling upon Jupiter, use a different deity with whom you feel more comfortable.

Materials: an elevated outdoor space where you can sit for a while, such as the top of a hill; something comfortable to sit or lie on; a tent with an open screened area set up to face the south (optional); a compass; a libation such as wine or juice; serene flute music (optional); incense and a lighter (optional); a bird identification guide; Book of Shadows or journal; a writing tool; a watch or timepiece.

Once you find a location you wish to use for the ornithomancy, use the compass to determine the cardinal directions. Draw a line in the ground before you from east to west, which represents the path the sun takes. Draw another line from north to south. These lines define the four quadrants.

Set yourself up facing south with the crossroads directly before you. If you're in a tent, align the edge of your tent to be parallel with the east-to-west line. Drink to Jupiter and pour some wine on the ground while extolling his virtues. You may light incense at this time, if you wish. Explain your request for the augury and ask for a yes or no answer via the birds. Discuss your field of vision, using visual landmarks such as trees or fences. This ensures the flight will be visible. Finally, ask for a confirmation that Jupiter will send a message through the birds for you to interpret. Your request might look something like this:

Mighty Jupiter, expansive one,

Lord of the Sky and Thunder,

I offer you this wine and fine rosemary incense.

I call upon your wisdom and assistance.

Benevolent one, please tell me—

Will my handfasting with Firi be successful?

I ask you to send me a clear sign through the birds,

your messengers, that will tell me yes or no.

I will look for your signs from the lilac bush on my left

to the maple tree on my right.

I will sit for three hours.

Will you do this for me, O powerful one?

Once you receive a positive response that Jupiter will send the sign, sit and watch the sky. Enter a trance state or practice the Air Vessel Meditation in Chapter 11. Remain silent without interruption for your predetermined amount of time. If desired, more incense may be burned and flute music can be played—it's thought that these please Jupiter and draw the birds out.

Write down all of the birds you see and what they do. Every bird you see and its activity are significant. For example, there's a huge difference between a cardinal that appears and leaves immediately and a cardinal that sings in the branches of the maple tree for an extended period of time. The former could be interpreted as a sign of illusory happiness, and the latter a sign of actual happiness and family. Use your watch and your Book of Shadows or journal to record what's happening and how long it happens.

When the viewing period is over, interpret the omens using the information about birds in this chapter. You may receive one clear message or several messages, which may be mixed. If your message is unclear, talk about it with a trusted friend who may be able to provide additional insights.

Fancy Flights

If you've ever worked with these creatures up close, you've probably felt the wild, raw power emanating from them. These animals have deep archetypal powers that can assist you greatly in your magical workings. Simply being near them is deeply moving and inspiring. Allow yourself to be uplifted by these majestic wonders of flight.

PART
3

RECIPES, RITUALS
& SPELLCRAFT

*Magick is a convenient word
for a whole collection of techniques,
all of which involve the mind.*

—MARGOT ADLER, DRAWING DOWN THE MOON

Chapter 9

THE MAGIC OF INCENSE

Incense is one of the most accessible and pleasurable tools of the element of air. The history of incense goes back to the first people who ever burned fragrant wood or herbs in their fires and marveled at the aromatic smells. Perhaps unsurprisingly, our sense of smell is one of the oldest senses we have. Smell is a unique sense because it skips the part of the brain that's responsible for processing. Instead, it travels directly to a more reactive place called the olfactory bulb, where there's a bank of stored emotions and memories. This area houses all of the links between the aromas and emotions that we create in our lifetimes as well as others that we may have inherited from our ancestors. In other words, whenever we burn the same fragrant woods or incense our ancestors would have used, we're likely to evoke our own memories and those of our ancestral past.

Incense use was first recorded in some of the oldest documents known to humankind. Babylonians, Mesopotamians, and South Asians wrote about its multitude of purposes around 3100 BCE. Likewise, one account of an ancient Egyptian village reported that, at night, incense smoke wafted into the air from all of the

CHAPTER 9

homes and temples in the entire neighborhood. The smoke from burning incense was likened to mystical clouds that linger around hilltops and mountaintops, which happens to be where several of the earliest known pagan deity altars were located.

This chapter covers the many uses of incense and gives several suggestions on how to use it. Of course, safety is an important consideration. Don't leave burning incense unattended, and be sure to place it where it won't come into contact with anyone, including pets. Research the effects of incense on you, your family, and your pets before burning. Beware of hot items like cauldrons or censers, and use heat-safe coasters beneath them to prevent damage. Always use metal tongs or a spoon to move charcoal or incense on charcoal. Never burn incense in a fire-sensitive area.

Although there are many precautions to take when using incense, in my opinion, it's worth it. The heavenly fumes support all kinds of air magic purposes.

Common Incenses

One of the primary reasons why incense is so alluring is because it releases the plant's essence or spirit into the air. The organic matter is transformed through fire into smoke, aromas, energy, and ash. Whenever we inhale the scents, they have the power to change us. We can choose different kinds of incense to suit our desired moods—it's extremely helpful to be more aligned with our magical purposes, to create a different mindset, or to facilitate an elevated, spiritual sense.

All incense corresponds with the element of air, even those plants that are associated with other elements. As you read through the different kinds of incense below, imagine that you're inhaling their aromas. Make note of the ones that spark your interest and check the index of this book to see if they're associated with air. If so, there'll be additional information about their specific properties that can aid you in your air magic.

Herbs

Rosemary, sage, mugwort, thyme, rue, lavender, rose, patchouli, gotu kola, lemongrass, vervain, jasmine, yerba santa, hops, chamomile, dandelion root, bay laurel, damiana, yarrow, elecampane, clover blossoms, mint, catnip, wormwood, vanilla, fern, heather, eucalyptus, eyebright, marshmallow root, fennel, angelica root, valerian root, lotus, sweetgrass, parsley

Spices

Anise seeds, cinnamon, cardamom seeds, clove, ginger, galangal, nutmeg, mace, ginseng, black pepper, allspice

Woods (including needles, bark, wood, and berries)

Juniper, pine, spruce, cedar, aloe, willow, fir, sandalwood *(use economically if at all—it may be endangered)*

Resins

Frankincense, copal, myrrh, dragon's blood, mastic, pine, acacia, benzoin

Incense in Magic

Incense is a fine way to mask odors or repel insects, but when it comes to magical uses, it's absolutely brilliant. There are five main spiritual purposes of burning incense. You can use these piecemeal as needed, or you could use them in an incense ritual starting with cleansing, then using incense to evoke a specific feeling, offering incense to the gods or spirits, then meditation, and finally, divination.

Cleansing

Before any magical work is performed, incense is often used to cleanse a ritual space and the magical practitioners. The smoke neutralizes any negative or stagnant energy, elevates the space energetically, and enables the magical element of air to come through more easily.

To cleanse a room for ritual, light incense and waft smoke around. Cleanse yourself first by wafting the smoke over your head and chest, then over your torso, legs, and feet (including the soles). Once your front side is cleansed, move the smoke over your backside as well, starting at the ankles and working your way up.

Cleanse the room by starting at the most commonly used doorway. Waft the smoke over all four corners of the door and finish by wafting smoke over the middle. Walk in a counterclockwise circle around the room along the walls, being sure to get the smoke into the corners of the room and the windows. When you're done, waft smoke onto the floor, the ceiling, and in the middle of the space.

Once you and the room are ready, you can cleanse any new magical tools or altar items by holding them over the smoke. If you work with other participants, cleanse them before they enter the room.

Evoking a Specific Feeling

Consider using scents in magical workings to create a specific mindset or mood that supports your work. Some covens and circles always use the same incense when they start a ritual because it effortlessly transports their minds and spirits to an otherworldly state.

Every ingredient in an incense blend carries a certain energy or tone. Consider what feeling you wish to conjure when you burn incense. For example, copal resin has a sweet, sacred scent, which is a very different aroma compared to the pungent, herbaceous smell of lavender flowers. They each set a different mood and have different purposes. If you're uncertain about what feeling you wish to evoke, take a whiff of what you have on hand. You'll probably be able to figure out which one will support your desired energy the most. The nose truly does know.

Offering to the Gods or Spirits

Incense carries our thoughts, wishes, and prayers to the elemental realm of air and spirits. Through the transformation of plant matter into smoke and energy, we give the gods and spirits energy, which they can use to assist us in our intentions and goals. Offerings to the gods and spirits were considered by many ancient cultures to be the only way to communicate with them, and incense has always been thought of as one of the best offerings.

If you wish to evoke a deity or a spirit, use the appropriate incense to do so. For example, if you know that Aphrodite likes rose incense, light it for her and set it on her altar. Use the same rose incense whenever you call upon her to form a bond between the two of you. If you don't know what kind of incense your deity or spirit likes, do some research, or simply ask them.

Meditation

Meditation doesn't require incense, but it can be burned to cultivate and sustain a spiritual mindset for as long as you wish to meditate. During meditation, the aroma of the incense encourages deep breathing, which induces a more relaxed body state. Use meditation in magical practices to cultivate a higher energetic state, such as a trance.

Divination

Incense has a long historical association with divination. Certain plants such as anise, mugwort, nutmeg, lavender, parsley, thyme, and others can be burned to bring about a mystical or visionary mindset. To see if incense enhances your abilities, light some up and use tarot, runes, automatic writing, throwing bones, or whatever you use for divination.

Ways to Burn Incense

There are so many wonderful ways to burn incense. Each method has positive and negative aspects, which will be discussed in the passages below. I've found it's best to have a variety of incense on hand for different situations that may arise, as some are more appropriate than others. But no matter how you burn it, incense is bound to move you with its intoxicating aroma.

Incense Sticks

One of the most common forms of incense is the hand-rolled stick made from oils, resins, woods, herbs, and sometimes, a filament made of bamboo or sandalwood. To use it, simply light the end, let it burn for a few seconds, and blow it out. If you see an ember, you'll know it's lit. It's generally used with an incense burner made of wood, metal, or ceramic with a hole in it to insert the incense. A variation of incense sticks is spiral incense, which is made in a similar manner.

The downside of incense sticks is that it's impossible to know exactly what's in them. This means you won't be able to look up the magical properties of ingredients. This isn't desirable for anyone who wants to connect with the plants they're burning, but it's especially bothersome if you have allergies. Sticks may contain artificial ingredients, hidden ingredients, or plants that are close to what's on the label, but not quite accurate. Lastly, you may not know if you're using an endangered plant like sandalwood. Whenever possible, choose reputable brands that are more likely to list accurate ingredients.

Incense sticks have so many positive aspects—they're easy to burn, relatively safe, and as long as the burner catches the ashes, they're a neat way to enjoy aromas. They're also inexpensive and easily procurable, as they are a commonly stocked form of incense. Incense sticks are perfect if you're a beginner or if you want a steady stream of aroma that you can light and not have to tend.

Incense Cones

Incense cones are another variation of prepared incense. Like incense sticks, they're made with plant matter and may contain oils, fragrance, and activated charcoal as well. To use these, simply light the top of the cone until a glowing ember forms, then blow it out. Set it in a cauldron or on a fireproof dish such as one made of ceramic. Incense cones have the same benefits and drawbacks as incense sticks, only they're a little more difficult to find.

Incense Charcoal

If you want to experience a wide variety of incense, charcoal is the way to go. It's the best method for burning essential oils and resins, and it's the preferred method for wood and herbs that have been finely chopped or ground. Many people feel this method gives a more direct connection with the plants, as you can see the materials in their raw form before they're burned on the charcoal. This method also lets you design your own aromas and change them as you see fit.

Incense charcoal is available at a variety of places, including some Witch shops. You'll also need to procure metal tongs and a metal censer or a cauldron. Your cauldron or censer doesn't need to be large—in fact, the ones that are just big enough for a disk of charcoal will do. If you're concerned about damaging your cauldron or censer, use a layer of sand beneath the charcoal.

When you want to burn charcoal incense, unwrap a charcoal disk and hold it using the tongs. Touch it to a flame of a candle—I recommend a candle because it can take a few seconds to catch. Watch for sparks racing across the disk, followed by a red glowing ember. Once you're sure the charcoal is lit, put it in the cauldron or censer. Allow it to sit and fully ignite for a moment before adding anything to it.

Once your charcoal disk is ready, sprinkle a little bit of incense onto the disk. Charcoal will burn just about any kind of incense. For the best results, grind your incense down to a powder and sprinkle it on, or use smaller items. Essential oils can be dropped onto burning incense charcoal for a burst of aroma. However, a little goes a long way, so use caution at first. Using too much essential oil could also extinguish the charcoal. Incense usually burns for a few minutes before the plant matter is gone. When it stops smoking, add more incense, if desired.

Burning incense this way is especially nice if you want to control how much incense is burning at one time. You can make the aromas more intense by adding more, or reduce the intensity by removing some with metal tongs. If you wish to change the aroma, use the tongs to scrape off what's currently burning and add something else. This method also gives you more certainty over what you're burning so you can enjoy the aromas without worrying about artificial fragrances that show up in incense sticks sometimes.

The downside of this method is that it requires a lot of attention if you like a steady stream of smoke. There's also a delicate balance with the charcoal—too much material on the disk will extinguish it, and too little will give you barely any smoke at all. You'll also have to keep the charcoal in a bag to keep moisture out, which could deactivate it.

Burning Raw Herbs and Woods

If you prefer to work with raw materials, try using a large cauldron or a metal bowl. This method works especially well with medium-sized whole pieces of herbs like bay, sage, and rosemary; or woods like pine, juniper, and sandalwood.

To burn raw materials as incense, light the plant matter on fire and drop it directly into the bowl or cauldron. Let it burn at its own pace. This method of incense keeps the cauldrons and bowls cool enough to hold by their handle or at their base. You can waft the smoke with your hand or a feather, if you wish. If your bowl or cauldron is big enough, keep a small tea light or votive candle inside it. Having the flame so close to the burning incense makes lighting and relighting it easy. In low lighting, it also creates a mysterious and dazzling effect, as both smoke and light pour from the cauldron.

The best thing about this method is that you can burn what you have on hand instantly—there's little to no preparation needed. Another benefit is that, because you experience the plant in its raw form, it's easy to develop a strong understanding of its nature before it burns. The downside of this method is that it's a potential fire hazard, particularly for anyone who wears long sleeves of a flammable material. Another downside is that this method can't be used for oils, resins, or finely chopped or ground items.

Outdoor Considerations

If you have the ability to burn incense outdoors, there are a few fun things you can do with it. You could toss herbs or woods directly into a bonfire. It creates a dramatic flair to any ritual or outdoor party, but there's less control over where the smoke goes, and the scent may be short-lived. Incense sticks are usually a good method for outdoor events. Another idea is to try a larger-scale variation of the charcoal method: place several lit incense charcoals in a large heat-proof container and sprinkle herbs or resins in them every now and then. This lets you burn massive amounts of incense at once. Depending on what you burn, it may even keep insects away.

Incense Tips

You may want to grind your incense into smaller material so it will burn more evenly. A heavy mortar and pestle are usually better than a lightweight one. As you crush the herbs or resin, connect with the essence of the plant. Use a dedicated mortar and pestle for grinding incense to prevent potentially contaminating your food.

When purchasing incense, try to choose items that were sustainably harvested. A great way to accomplish this is to grow your own plants if possible. I recommend using the purest ingredients, including herbs and resins, whenever possible. Look for incense sticks made with essential oils and plant matter as opposed to ones made from dung and artificial fragrances (if you're sensitive to them). If possible, use "green" charcoal incense made from a sustainable substance like bamboo.

Many prepared incense sticks and cones contain a blend of ingredients. For example, some incense producers sell an incense blend called "Air," with ingredients that vary widely from one manufacturer to the next. It's my opinion that you don't *have* to know what all the ingredients are before buying incense; however, I recommend smelling it before purchasing to ensure you'll like the smell.

Whenever you light up incense, give silent thanks to the spirit of the plant for its contribution to your magic and awareness. If you want to add extra potency to your air magic, ask it to facilitate an air power such as knowledge, discernment, change, wisdom, communication, or connection with spirits. This helps you connect with the plant and makes the burning of incense more sacred.

Another idea is to recite an incantation over the incense to put your energy and intentions into it. Envision the results of what will happen when you burn it in a ritual or in magical work. When you eventually do burn the incense, you'll experience that same sensation when it's transformed into pure essence and energy. Envision the incense spreading far and wide along with your magic.

Incense Smoke Divination, or Libanomancy

Avlelio Mato Watakpe is a devotee of Santa Muerte, a Hermetic Qabalist, and a modern day eclectic cunning-man. He is a full-time spellworker, oracle, writer, and teacher of the Occult; he incorporates folk Native American rootwork, Hellenic polytheism, Solomonic magick, and traditions found in the grimoires of old into his magick and practice.

THE ART AND practice of incense smoke divination have long been known as libanomancy. With records of this form of prophetic interpretation dating from 2000 to 1600 BCE in Babylonia, and with libanomancy also noted as a deeply honored tool of the oracles at Delphi, it has been a revered divinatory method throughout the ages. It is generally performed by casting loose herbal incenses, powders, and mixtures onto burning coals or charcoal discs; and observing and interpreting the speed and movements of the smoke, images and shapes in it, and the sounds, smells, and even tastes that the smoke produces.

Before you begin, ensure that all airflow has been halted to the best of your ability, as the direction the smoke travels is one of the most important factors. As with any form of divination, it's good to have a clear and specific question as well as an open mind.

MATERIALS

    loose herbal incense or powder

    incense charcoal

    censer or cauldron

    lighter

    camera (optional)

Light the charcoal disk and burn the incense. If the incense burns quickly and has no disruptions or difficulties as it begins, and the smoke initially rushes directly upward in large plumes, it is incredibly auspicious and fortunate, as you have made direct contact with the spirits. The same is true if there are pops and crackles throughout the burning of the incense, and it indicates communication and physical contact from the spirits to the diviner.

Smoke that moves toward you, especially if it does so quickly after it rises upward, is a powerful and positive affirmation of your motives, manifestations, or inquiry. Smoke that moves away from you in a similar manner is a decisively negative response, which shows that your endeavors will bear unwanted outcomes. Thick, clustered plumes of smoke are indicative of great success and a positive response to your inquiry. Fragmented smoke or thin columns shows that there are difficulties, and represents hardship. Slow-burning incense leading to small amounts of smoke, or none at all, shows that there is immense difficulty in your endeavors coming into materialization or experiential success, or that your goals may not manifest whatsoever. If at first, the smoke is thin and shows difficulty in igniting, but eventually turns to billowing plumes of smoke which quickly rises upward or toward you, it shows that there are some energetic blockages which you will eventually overcome, representing a positive yet troubled response.

Traditionally, it is said that if the smoke naturally flows to the left side, it is indicative of failure in your endeavors or a negative answer to your inquiry, and that smoke flowing to the right is indicative of success and positivity. While it may be helpful to keep these archaic concepts in mind, it is much more potent to interpret these directions in a broader sense, incorporating the widely-used occult understanding that the left side generally refers to feminine energies or qualities, and the right side to the masculine.

Through this attribution, you can relate left-flowing smoke to subconscious energies and natures, circumstances which are yet to manifest, deeply emotional energy which may carry the extremes of unwavering nurturing or terrible destruction, influences from the distant past, or other such qualities of the divine feminine. You can relate right-flowing smoke to the conscious will of the spirits and cosmic forces; your works and inquiries being blessed with spiritual activity and forcefulness; life-giving and penetrating energies; creative ingenuity; circumstances that are certain to be manifest positively, joyously, or victoriously; or other such qualities of the divine masculine.

Many diviners also look for shapes, images, and symbols in the smoke. Types of images that can be found include all types of animal spirits; faces or whole forms of spirits and deities; sigils and seals of various entities; Hebrew and Greek letters; Latin letters and numbers; attributes and symbols of deities; astrological symbols; runes; and classic occult imagery, such as the egg, wheel, heart, flame, chalice, blade, cross, snake, key, crown, or pentacle.

Technology has made discovering and interpreting the messages that come through incense smoke much easier. You can set up your phone or a DSLR camera on a stand facing your altar and record a video. Watch the footage as much as you may need, pausing where it is clear that you are receiving some sort of imagery. Additionally, many DSLR cameras can be set to take still-frame pictures every second or so, and there are otherwise accessories that enable almost any camera to have this feature. Alternatively, it does not hurt to pause during a divination, ritual, or spell-working, in order to snap several photos of the incense smoke. These methods give you many images to investigate and draw information from, so set up your devices and get to delving into the smoke!

Avlelio Mato Watakpe

• • • •

Up in Smoke

A common Egyptian saying is, "a day without fragrance is a day lost."[10] Whether you burn incense on your main altar, an incense table, or a shrine, know that it comes with a rich history of evocative emotions. With all of the different kinds of incense available to you in this chapter, you're bound to find something that inspires you.

Consider designing your own incense blend to evoke a specific mindset. It's fun to experiment with combinations of herbs, oils, and resins until you get it right. New fragrance blends can give you new mental associations, which may assist in healing the mind. Perhaps best of all, they can also allow you to bridge the gap between our world and the magical realm of air.

10 Thomas Kinkele, *Incense and Incense Rituals* (Twin Lakes: Lotus Press, 2005), 7.

159

Chapter 10

WINDS, SOUNDS, AND WORDS

Air is the medium through which so much travels. It transports energy in the form of wind, and it carries vibration waves that we perceive as sounds and words. Winds, sounds, and words give life and expression to the element of air. They can be utterly inspirational—for example, think of how a spirited breeze feels as it rushes past you. Imagine listening to your favorite song and feeling the goose bumps that rise up on the back of your neck when the music crests. Words of love from someone you care about can fill you with sublime energy and happiness. Allow these correspondences of the element of air to move you similarly and rouse your air magic to even greater heights.

Winds

Watching the skies is an ancient and mesmerizing practice. When air fronts collide and the winds pick up, the feeling of electricity in the air can build up so much that it feels like magic is at your fingertips, ready for your words. Weather Witches work with this type of energy. They also use their skills in aims to alter the weather.

History of Weather Magic

There's evidence of people all over the world performing rituals and magical practices to bring about their desired weather. The first known citation of weather magic was in the Greek epic poem *The Odyssey* from the eighth century BCE. Odysseus asked Aeolus, the ruler of the four winds, for assistance in sailing home. Aeolus gifted him the west wind in his sails as well as a bag of bound winds in the hide of an ox. In the fourth century BCE, the Greek philosopher Empedocles also used sacks of animal skin to catch the wind for his air magic. In his writings, he said there were many other cultures near Greece who knew weather magic too, likely Persians and the inhabitants of modern-day Romania and Bulgaria, but those transcripts have likely been lost to the centuries. Greek sailors regularly attempted weather magic, according to the ancient Greek epic poem *Argonautica*, from the third century BCE. They also made offerings and prayers to twin gods known as the Kabeiroi, who could make a storm blow over faster and calm the weather. The belief in weather witchery was so strong in the ancient world that a man was given the death penalty for binding winds that prevented ships from sailing into a Constantinople harbor in the third century CE.[11]

Wind magic was regularly practiced in Finland as well. Air Witches tied knots in rope that bound the powers of the wind, a practice that was first recorded in the 1300s. Sailors bought these enchanted ropes and unknotted them, one at a time, while at sea.

11   Sir James Frazier, *The Golden Bough: A Study in Magic and Religion*, abridged ed. (Macmillan, 1922; Bartlelby.com, 2000), https://www.bartleby.com/196/13.html, accessed September 9, 2019.

Each loosed knot released a more powerful gust of wind. This form of weather witchery must have been successful because the practice continued for centuries. Wind knots were still in demand in 1939, and they're thought to be used to this very day.

Weather magic made an appearance in Shakespeare's play *The Tempest* when the magician Prospero and his familiar Ariel create a storm to make a boat crash upon the shores of his island. Weather witchery also appears in *Macbeth*—the three Witches known as the Weird Sisters combine their winds to create a storm and sink a ship.

These days, weather magic is practiced by many Witches and magicians. It's regularly used to clear the skies at outdoor events such as festivals, weddings, performances, and games. Like regular magic, it's up to you to decide how you want to use it. Be safe and use common sense—if you see a strike of lightning, move your practice to a shelter. Wait at least thirty minutes after the last lightning strike to venture outside again. Be aware of the need for both sunshine and rain—too much of either one will damage crops and other vegetation. If it has been a while since the last hard rain, don't deter storms simply for the sake of wanting another sunny day.

General Weather Concepts

Weather witchery builds upon a few basic atmospheric concepts. Understanding these isn't essential, but knowing about these physical occurrences will definitely aid your understanding of how weather works.

Wind is the result of the sun's energy and the earth's rotation. As air currents move over the earth, they pick up whatever is below them, whether that's moisture from water or dust particles from the earth. You can always tell how much moisture is in the air by looking to see how many clouds are in the sky. If there are a lot of clouds close to the earth, the weight of water adds pressure to the air, which is measured with a barometer as low barometric pressure. Some sensitive people feel this as a building tension. It can feel oppressive, especially if there's no wind to relieve the energy. Some people may feel this pressure for several hours before another air front sweeps in and changes it. Conversely, when it's a sunny day, there's high barometric pressure. Many people sense this as a lighter mood with less weighing them down.

There are often several layers of air currents above our heads at any given time. It's possible to have stormy clouds close to the earth and sunny skies above. When two air fronts with different temperatures and moistures collide, the result is usually a thunderstorm, with an exchange of energy released in the forms of rain, thunder, wind, and lightning. Air currents may follow a seasonal pattern such as El Niño, or the air current may blow in from mostly one direction.

If you're just starting out with weather witchery, look at your local weather on a regular basis. Do this by going outside and assessing how the weather feels, using a weather app, tracking the weather online, or by paying attention to the weather reports on television. The Weather Channel is a particularly useful resource when it comes to weather witchery. If you prefer to venture outside, look at the clouds in the skies, their quantity, shape, and how high up they are. Ascertain which direction the weather is coming from by feeling which way the wind is blowing. Look for trends in the weather. Try to predict what weather will arrive in the next few hours based on what you see and feel and what's on the horizon.

When you have a baseline for what your local weather does on a regular basis, you can start to play with weather magic.

Move Air Currents With Your Mind

There are two general ways to move air currents. The first is pushing air masses, and the other is pulling them. These all involve working with the thermodynamics at hand and envisioning what you want to happen. If you've used reiki before and know how to direct energy, you'll have a head start.

One of the best things a weather Witch can do is part the clouds, especially at an outdoor pagan or witchcraft festival. It's relatively easy, and it only takes a moment. Focus on your core and see a ball of fiery energy in your body. Hold it in your hands and feel how hot and dry it is. Slowly lift it to the skies and release it. Envision it traveling up, drying up the clouds, and making way for the sun.

The next time it rains and you're not in the mood for drizzles, try making the storm go off-course. Push the storm in one direction by creating a mass of air in your hands that has the same temperature and moisture content. Hold it for a moment, then direct it to the sky in the direction you want the storm to go. This pushes it away from you, at least for a little while. If the storm has a built-up train of storm clouds behind it, you'll need to continue this action.

Another form of parting the clouds and averting storms involves the projection of an ethereal structure in the sky in the shape of a diamond or a kite. Position a long, narrow tip toward the oncoming weather, just beneath the clouds. Imagine that the structure has a body that rises up and flares out to cover the area in need of protection. The clouds will part at the tip of the structure and go to either side of it.

You can also try your mind at pulling air pockets toward you. For example, if you want cloud cover and it's sunny, imagine you have an ethereal hand that pulls the clouds closer to you. This speeds them along on their course and alters their course a little too.

Many times, weather magic can yield surprisingly successful results. Though of course, there are times when a storm's energy is far greater than yours. Sometimes it just has to rain, and no amount of willpower or thinking about clear skies can change that.

Weather witchery may seem difficult at first, but keep practicing. With time, it comes with greater ease. As a young weather Witch, I remember straining to push air masses and feeling exhausted afterward. These days, all I do is mentally project my energy into the skies with the intention that it will push the air masses. Experiment with trying hard and using your will, and then try using the power of your mind. A combination of techniques may give you the best outcome.

Absorb the Energy of the Weather

Absorptive weather magic involves absorbing the energy from whatever weather is occurring. This could be anything from a sunny day, a snowstorm, windy days, a storm, or any other weather. The harder the wind, the greater physical air energy there will be for you to draw upon. You can also use humidity, electricity, or the pressure in the air. Each of these will influence the energy you absorb.

To absorb the energy of the weather, stand in it or adjacent to it, such as in a house with the window open. Increase your breathing and focus on being in the present moment. Experience the atmospheric conditions as much as you can. Feel the wind on your face and body, the heat (or lack thereof), the humidity (or lack thereof), and the energy. Notice if the weather makes any sounds, such as whooshing through the tree branches or whistling around the corner of a building. More than anything, feel the energy of the weather.

Inhale deeply and draw these sensations into yourself. Pull in their energy and let it come into your body. Extend your sensations outside of yourself to feel additional energy such as the electricity in the air. Connect with it all and draw even more into yourself.

When you've reached a maximum capacity, direct the energy. The energy could be used in a ritual at that moment for manifestation and be released with your intention. It could be used for any kind of air magic, such as summoning a spirit. It could also be used for other weather magic—for example, you could absorb the energy of a storm and direct that energy back into the skies to push the storm in another direction. You can store the energy in a crystal or an amulet by envisioning light flowing from your hands into it. This stores the energy for later use, like a battery. Use this method for general mood improvement or when you want to call upon the magical element of air in a ritual.

When you're done with the magical working, release any additional weather energy to the air around you by exhaling completely and wiggling your body. Take a cleansing breath to draw in fresh energy. If necessary, ground the energy by placing your hands on the earth and releasing it.

Wind Knots

Like the sea Witches, you too can tie up the wind in knots. These are particularly useful when you want to change the current weather into something else. Traditionally, sea Witches tied one knot for a gale, a second knot for a stronger wind, and a third for a storm. However, you can tie up the energy of whatever breezes you have nearby. All you need is a blustery day and a rope or ribbon that's at least twelve inches in length.

Go outside and stand in the wind so that it flows from behind you and over you. It's best if there's nothing behind you to block the wind from moving around you. Let the rope or ribbon dangle in the wind. Tie the first knot and envision the energy of the wind being bound by the rope or ribbon while saying, "I bind you, wind, into this knot." As long as the wind is still blowing, you can tie additional ones using the same imagery. Store the wind knots on your air altar.

When you wish to release the wind from the knots, untie them a little at a time while saying, "I free you, wind, from this knot." Imagine the energy flowing out of the knot and being free.

Shrines for the Four Winds

If you feel connected with the magical element of air, you could make shrines to each of the four directional winds. Several cultures from all over the world worked with these four winds. The belief in them is thought to supersede the classic view of the four elements.

If you wish, you can use the meanings of the four winds from a specific culture, such as Greek, Roman, Celtic, or Norse. Or designate your own meanings. Figure out the significances of the four cardinal winds at your location by watching the weather and observing the qualities of the winds.

Where I live, the wind from the west brings most of my weather, so I associate the west wind with "going with the flow." The wind that comes from the north is often cool. It's sometimes rainy or snowy, but predictably so. The north wind, for me, represents coolness and a regular change in the normal pattern. Wind from the south is usually warm and tropical, and it sometimes brings violent weather, like hurricanes. To me, this is like the fiery, strong aspect of air. Wind from the east is sporadic and seems to be slightly chaotic. For me, the east wind is the instigator of unexpected changes and champion of underdogs.

Call upon the individual winds you need when you desire their unique energies, or invite multiple winds for big magic. Calling upon the winds does *not* mean you're asking them to blow as much as possible. You're merely bringing their presence and energy to you. In other words, as long as you're not asking for all of the winds to blow fiercely at the same time, you don't have to worry about creating a tornado. If you like working with the four winds, consider making shrines to them or give them physical placeholders such as stones, if possible.

Sound

Sound and music are universal languages that everyone understands. Druids believed that music, specifically singing, was so powerful that it could heal wounds. The Navajo Native American tribespeople believe this too—their curing ceremonies take the form of a song. Music sets a specific tone and energy. The right kind of music can easily clear away negative energy and shift the frequency of a ritual space toward your intended focus.

Sacred Sounds in Magic

Sacred sounds that correspond with the element of air include chimes, bells, singing bowls, and singing. You can create these sounds yourself, or play recorded sounds. Experiment with them to find ones that produce the right style for your magical workings. You may also want to consider having more than one bell, chime, or bowl. A pleasant, high-pitched note is good for higher vibrational work and rituals that involve spiritual energy, such as manifestation. A deep, resonant tone is better for lower vibrational magic such as physical or emotional work.

Bells

Before my rituals, I often use a bell to cleanse my space. As the sound of the bell rings out, I imagine the vibrations and sound clearing the space energetically. After casting a circle, I ring the bell again to set the focus and tone. It's also nice to use after a particularly heavy ritual to lighten the mood. When I'm done with the magical working and I've opened the circle, I ring the bell one last time to clear out any remaining energy. In group rituals, ringing a bell can also be an effective way to cut chatter, focus attention, and get everyone to shift to the next part of the ritual.

Wind Chimes

Another air-related instrument is wind chimes because they're moved by the wind. These are great because they acknowledge wind and the element of air, sometimes when you least expect it. There's nothing quite like standing on a porch with the wind blowing and the sounds of wind chimes ringing out. It feels exciting and uplifting, as if anything could happen. I've always had wind chimes at the various places I lived because their pleasant sounds made my apartment or house feel more like a home.

Other Musical Instruments

Although many instruments can represent air, some are more airy than others. Wind instruments, or ones that use breath to make music, all correspond with the element of air—for example, the flute, oboe, clarinet, recorder, and pan pipes. Listening to music from these instruments can open your mind more, increase mental abilities, help with visualization, and promote psychic powers.

Spoken Word

Words are powerful. They create opportunities and bonds, but they can just as easily cut or destroy them. The spoken word is considered by many people to be the most important air tool of them all. Whether you whisper words to yourself, speak them aloud with ferocity, or use sign language, words are the most direct form of communication and expression. They evoke images and energies. Every time we speak, we're claiming what we want and calling that energy to come to us. This is true in our everyday lives and in ritual.

The word *abracadabra* is thought to translate to, "I create as I speak." In other words, without speaking, there would be no creation. Likewise, some magicians believe that magical works that are performed without words are nearly impotent. Related to this concept is the Japanese belief that every word carries its own mystical powers, some with powers of creation, and some with powers of destruction. Many people believe the gods and spirits wait for us to speak our desires into the air so they can change our worlds in that manner.

Power of the Spoken Word

Once, when I was about nine years old, I sat in a packed auditorium with about three hundred other kids at a day-long space camp. That morning and afternoon, we had spoken with astronauts, engineers, and scientists about the work they did.

Finally, it was the moment we were all waiting for—the big raffle at the end of the day. With prizes like a hot air balloon trip or a flight in a World War II fighter jet, the tension in the auditorium was palpable. Row after row of kids leaned closer to hear the organizers call the names of the winners. Everyone clapped as, one after another, the winners walked onto the stage.

In no time, they'd called out six names, and mine was not one of them. I scanned the winners, and when I noticed they were all boys, a wave of frustration rose within me. Girls made up about a third of the participants, but there weren't any girl winners at all. Anger flared up in my stomach.

The organizer announced the next prize—a trip in a jet—and rummaged for a raffle ticket in the bowl.

I couldn't stand it any longer. At the top of my lungs, I yelled, "pick a girl!" I was so loud that the kids sitting in the row in front of me startled and turned around to gape at my audacity.

I bet you can guess what happened next. The organizer pulled a raffle ticket out, and whose name was announced over the speaker?

Mine. My face flushed with hot embarrassment, but I stood up and made my way toward the stage through a sea of astonished faces.

Although it's possible that I would've won the prize if I hadn't shouted my desires into a packed auditorium, I like to think that the power of the spoken word and my passionate state made magic happen that day.

The Hidden Link Between Belief and Words

We need to pay attention to the words we use about ourselves and our abilities. The words we speak create so much of what we perceive as possible in our lives. If you talk negatively about yourself, take a hint from the magical element of air and make a change. Decide to speak better about yourself starting this very moment. When you support yourself like a friend would, you'll get a lot further in life because there'll be less self-sabotage. It only takes a little bit of regular training to replace negative words with positive or neutral ones. A phrase like, "I could never do that," becomes, "I would love to learn how to do that!" Thoughts like, "I'm a hot mess today," become "I'm phenomenally wonderful in my own way."

Ultimately, what we say about ourselves reveals a deeper truth: how much we believe in ourselves. Fortunately, belief is another power of the element of air. It may be that both your beliefs and your expressions need to be evaluated.

Voice

Another aspect of the spoken word is the voice. When I first called upon a deity or a spirit, I remember my voice quavering. I wasn't used to this form of communication. My voice did the same thing when I spoke my first affirmations and intentions aloud. Asking for what I wanted was foreign to me, and it didn't come easily. With time, I was able to use my voice with more authority and power. Learning how to express myself has taken a long time to master, but it's a journey that I'm so glad I started on.

It's important to have a voice that matches how you feel you project yourself in the world. No one can control their genetic features, like the shape of a mouth or a throat, but efforts can be made to enunciate more, reduce nasality, turn up or down your volume, or use the diaphragm to make a voice sound less swallowed. If you want to develop your spoken word skills, consider seeing a speech therapist or joining a public speaking organization. The skills you learn in just a few hours may give you more confidence to believe in the power of your words and use them when you want.

Having a powerful voice isn't about conforming to normalcy or having a "perfect accent." This is about having a voice that represents you. When you identify with your voice, and you believe in the power of it, it resonates with others. When you want to use it, you'll be less intimidated—you'll speak up for yourself and others more often. You'll use your voice as a tool for change and positive growth.

Through the Air

The magical powers of wind, sound, and words have been recognized for a very long time. They're just as important and effective now, in our modern age, as they were then. Some of these magical studies may take longer to master than others. However, claiming more agency over them elevates our inner and outer under-standings. So, breathe in the wind and let it inspire you. Use your voice and mean what you say. Let the power of sounds elevate your magic. These powers of air are at your command.

Chapter 11

AIRY MEDITATIONS, SPELLS, AND RITUALS

Magic travels at the speed of thought. With our minds, breath, and words, we communicate our wishes to the magical element of air. The invisible winds take this energy and transmit it far and wide, influencing things in our favor.

Because air is the most transmissive element, be aware of the air around you during your magical practices. It may change to feel warmer or cooler, heavier or lighter, or tingly and electric. Sometimes, the abundance of energy and power in a magical practice can make you feel as if you're walking through a dense fog. When this happens, it's an indicator that a shift in energy has occurred.

The magical practices in this chapter were chosen because they bring more presence to one's relationship with the energy of air. Additional air correspondences can be added to your magic to increase the energy available to you and add specific meanings.

For the meditations in this chapter, consider recording them and playing them back to get the full benefit. Whenever you finish a ritual, ground back into your body by drinking water and eating a little bit of food. You may want to lie down or relax—I suggest cuddling those you love, reading a book, meditating, sleeping, or watching a good show on television. Follow your intuition when it comes to the post-ritual care you need.

Magic to Get In Touch with the Element of Air
Air Vessel Meditation

This empowering meditation aligns the body and mind with the magical element of air. By bringing pure air energy inside the body, you connect with air's expansiveness, spirituality, aspects of change, communication, inspiration, and any other air attributes you want to bring about. I use this technique to ensure my mindset is appropriate before any air magic, such as spirit work or weather witchery.

Begin by closing your eyes. Take a few deep breaths. With each exhalation, release your thoughts and emotions. Imagine your thoughts and emotions are particles inside of you. Every breath releases them into the air, making your energy purer. With every inhalation, breathe in the magical element of air. Envision this as a stimulating and uplifting energy that makes the energy inside of your body even clearer. Continue breathing until you feel a sublime shift.

Imagine that you are a vessel filled with the magical element of air. You may envision this as a translucent energy within your body, or you may envision yourself as a clear vase filled with swirling air. Continue breathing deeply and fill your vessel with even more energy. When you reach an apex of how much air energy you can handle, maintain it for a moment or two, feeling the magical air inside of you. Meditate on being the vessel as long as you wish.

When you want to return your consciousness to a more grounded state, exhale any extraneous air energy you no longer need while remembering to keep a little for yourself. If you need additional grounding, envision your body is connected with the energy of the earth. Place your hands on your body or the earth, or hold a grounding stone such as hematite. With time and practice, you'll be able to channel this energy with greater ease to use it whenever you need it.

Magical Breath Wish Spell

Whenever you combine the personal and the magical qualities of the element of air, you can transform your breath from a basic, everyday task into magical breath. This can be used for trance work and meditation, to cleanse objects, to charge objects, and to transmit your desires into the world. One of the most common ways people use magical breath is the birthday wish. Fortunately, you don't have to wait for your solar return. I recommend using a cupcake with this spell to make the moment extra special, but a candleholder will work just as well.

MATERIALS

    birthday candle

    lighter

    candleholder or a cupcake

Light the candle, turn off the lights, and gaze at the flame. Think about how far you've come in the past year and where you'd like to go. Sing a song—nearly any song will do, but it should be empowering. As you sing, call upon the magical element of air within you. Hear the sounds of your words and picture them changing the air around you with their sound waves. Continue to sing until you feel your energy rise.

Close your eyes and speak your wish in your mind. Take as much time as you need to get it right. When you're ready, open your eyes and blow out the candle with your magical breath. Envision this breath dispersing your wish to the four winds that blow all over the world. Eat the cupcake and celebrate your wish coming true.

Wind Cleansing Spell

There's something so energizing about being outside on a windy day. It always inspires me to release that which I don't need. For this spell, you can wait for a breeze to arrive, or you can go to a windy place, such as a hill, ridge, or a large body of water. You could even do this in the car with the windows down if you're not driving.

MATERIALS

a windy location

When the wind picks up, breathe it in. Feel it touch your clothing, body, hair, and skin. When you feel a connection with the element of air, speak the words:

Mighty wind, cleanse me.

Take away the energy I willingly shed.

Let it travel away from me,

far away, never to be seen again.

Imagine the wind blowing through you and cleansing you to an energetic level. Release anything that feels like it wants to leave you—simply let it go. Envision anything you don't need flowing away from you on the wind.

Wind Chime Spell for Happiness

You can use the power of the wind in your magic even when you're not around. In this spell, wind chimes enact the magic of happiness whenever the wind blows.

MATERIALS

> wind chimes in cheerful tones
> neroli essential oil

Go outside with your chimes and anoint them with neroli oil. Take a deep breath in and focus on what happiness feels like for you. Anoint each chime and the clapper and the sail in the middle.

Hold the chimes in the air and say:

Mighty element of air, be with me!
Enchant these chimes with the energy of pure happiness!
Every time the wind blows, may this
magic be renewed and good cheer spread.

Hold the chimes in the air until the wind makes them chime. Give thanks to the wind and hang them somewhere that will catch the wind often.

Magic for Mental Powers

Tea Spell for a Sharp Mind

If you want more focus, a good cup of tea can go a long way. This simple spell uses herbs known to clarify the mind and increase blood flow to the brain. Although it doesn't contain caffeine, it's so mentally stimulating that I don't recommend drinking it within an hour of bedtime.

Materials

> peppermint
>
> ginkgo
>
> gotu kola
>
> hyssop
>
> sage
>
> eyebright
>
> lemongrass
>
> bowl for mixing herbs
>
> tea kettle
>
> teapot
>
> spoon (silver if possible)
>
> teacup in an empowering air color associated with the mind such as purple, blue, or white.

Place the herbs and the bowl before you. One at a time, take a pinch of each herb and focus on its energy before dropping it into the bowl. When all the herbs are added, toss the tea in the air a little to stir them.

To prepare your tea, use a slightly rounded tablespoon for each twelve-ounce cup. While the tea is steeping, stir the tea clockwise with the silver spoon and recite the spell:

> *Magical tea, with every sip*
> *I call upon wisdom, focus, and wit.*
> *Insights, intelligence, clarity,*
> *Analysis, discernment, ability.*

Bless my mind with the strengths of air.

May it be so, as I declare!

Take a deep breath of the steam through your nose. Draw the warm energy inside you and direct it to clear your mind. When the tea is cool enough to drink, feel the positive energy strengthen your mind.

Charm Bag Spell for Positive Thoughts

This charm bag is so uplifting—the herbs and crystals ease worries and let you rise above. The fragrance stays for quite some time, and one whiff can elevate the mind to more positive dimensions.

MATERIALS

daisy

eyebright

basil

marjoram

mint

clear quartz

apophyllite

fluorite

bowl

a square of cloth in a happy color, approximately the size of your palm

string or yarn long enough to close the bag and possibly use it as a necklace

peppermint oil

Hold each of the herbs and crystals and connect with their spirits, then add them to the bowl. When all are added, mix them with your right pointer finger and say:

Negative thoughts, be gone from me.

I am now blessed with positivity.

As I will it, so shall it be.

Place the mixture on the square of cloth and put three drops of peppermint oil on the mixture. Inhale deeply and feel the aroma cleanse and uplift your mind. Tie the bag closed with nine knots to represent the wisdom to choose positive thoughts.

Ritual for Objectivity

This ritual uses the alchemical symbol of air and imagery from the ancient Egyptian pyramids. The bases of Egyptian pyramids contain the dead and all their belongings. The golden tops of the pyramids were for a different purpose—they had hieroglyphs of the *benu*, the phoenix-like bird that symbolizes transformation, rebirth, spirituality, and rising above earthly matters.

MATERIALS

    sage

    bay

    lemongrass

    hyssop

    mint

    summer savory

    incense charcoal and censer

    lighter

piece of paper

pen

Grind the incense together while focusing on gaining more objectivity in your life. Light the incense. As it burns, write down the thoughts or images that replay in your mind. For example, you might write, "stuck, hopeless, and empty." Draw the lower half of the symbol of air. This is shaped like an isosceles trapezoid or a triangle with its top cut off.

With its four sides, this shape carries the energy of the number 4, which is connected with conscientiousness, groundedness, and growth. However, when aspected poorly, it can represent harsh discipline, anger, judgment, an abundance of caution, resentment, working too hard, and a heavy energy. This represents where you are at this moment and everything you wish to rise above. Trace the shape four times while thinking of the list of things you wrote down. When you are ready to gain objectivity, put down the pen, take a deep breath, and recite the spell:

With every breath, I rise above
These useless thoughts I do not love.

Take a deep breath and inhale the incense smoke. Bring the magical element of air into your mind and feel your energy start to rise.

Pick up your pen again and draw the upper part of the symbol of air (a triangle) above the trapezoid. With three sides, the triangle and the number three are associated with happiness, strength, objectivity, communication, generosity, mental clarity, playfulness, wittiness, and creativity. Cross out the first things you wrote, and write down the opposite. For example, if you wrote "stuck, hopeless, empty," cross them out and write "free, inspired, full of life."

Trace the new triangle three times and say:

> *With insight, clarity,*
>
> *and abundant objectivity,*
>
> *I rise above those thoughts that bound me.*

Trace the entire symbol of the element of air five times. Five is the number of freedom, acuity, and active spiritual energy. It's also the number of points on a pyramid. Imagine looking down at your problems from a great height. Will these issues still bother you in a year? In five years? Say:

> *I now see with objectivity.*
>
> *Like the phoenix, elevated and free.*

Hang the paper over the incense smoke to seal in the symbol and your words. Let the incense burn out completely.

Magic for Communication

Power of the Spoken Word Spell

Too often, many people don't say what they really want. Speaking the truth of your desires out loud is powerful. It boosts your inner realization of that energy and helps you attract what you seek. This spell can be about attracting something, becoming something, or it can give you the courage to speak your truth aloud.

MATERIALS

lavender essential oil (diluted in a carrier oil)

sodalite

Anoint your throat with the lavender oil and place the sodalite stone on your neck. Take a few deep breaths and think about what you really want to say. Inhale deeply, bringing the magical element of air into your lungs. Speak aloud in a clear, strong voice for as long as you need. The energy of your words will travel into the magical plane of air, where they will begin to affect your body, mind, and spirit.

Spell to Bless the Tools of Communication

Communication often occurs with tools, such as pencils, pens, paper, microphones, phones, and computers. Blessing these tools can aid you in writing or speaking more eloquently. If you can't bring your desktop computer outside, bring your keypad.

MATERIALS

>   your communication tools
>
>   an aspen or an elder tree with leaves
>
>   a container of water from a spring, stream, or lake

Sit beneath the tree and lay out your tools so they're touching the trunk of the tree. Open the jar of water and pour it on the ground. Say:

> *With this water, mighty tree,*
>
> *I ask for blessings on all you see.*
>
> *May the right words come to me,*
>
> *just as air blows between your leaves.*

Wait until the wind blows, and remain for at least a few minutes. When it feels right to go, collect your belongings, give your thanks to the tree, and leave.

Creativity Candle Spell

Creativity is an elevated form of communication that includes thinking, planning, imagining, and focusing on ideas. It can take a lot of energy to sustain creative pursuits, especially at first. Fortunately, there are magical shortcuts. It's best to do creative work right after making the candle, but it will still work if you need to wait.

MATERIALS
>   pencil
>   paper
>   blue pillar candle with no glass
>   a carving knife
>   rosemary essential oil (diluted in a carrier oil)
>   lighter

With the pencil and paper, design a sigil for your creativity. It should express your creative products, goals, and how the creative arts make you feel. Carve the sigil into the middle of the candle, then spread the oil all over it while focusing on the energy of your sigil. Press your thumb to the sigil to activate it. Say:

May this candle sustain my creative energy!

May it give me inspiration and focus as long as it is lit.

Light the candle and start your creative work. Extinguish it when you stop working.

Magic for Change

Spell Jar to Create a New Beginning

This spell jar for a new beginning uses several correspondences of the element of air to initiate change in your life.

MATERIALS

    incense

    the Fool tarot card

    pine needles

    juniper berries

    vervain

    angelica

    salt

    sage

    frankincense

    clear quartz

    a small clipping of hair

    a jar

    scissors

    paper

    pencil

Light the incense and cleanse the Fool card, then set it down on your altar. Wash each ingredient in the incense smoke, touch them to the Fool card, and place them in the jar. Cut a piece of paper that will fit over the card. Cover the Fool card with the paper, and gently trace the lines of the card with the pencil. Draw one of your distinguishing features onto the Fool, such as a piece of your jewelry or your glasses. Place the drawing in the jar. Add incense smoke to the jar, then seal it shut. Bury the jar in the earth or in a potted plant as if you are planting a seed. For three weeks, water it every other day and tell it how much it's growing. On the fourth week, you can take the Fool card off your altar, confident in your new beginning.

Scatter Spell

This spell uses the wind to release the energies you no longer want. It's a powerful way to symbolically and literally move on. Due to the use of a pencil or marker, we recommend this spell not be done near or over a body of water.

Materials

>   flower petals or leaves (dried or fresh)
>   a fine-tipped marker or a pencil
>   athame (optional)

Go to a somewhat private location where you can release flower petals or leaves, preferably on the wind. The best place for this spell might be a section of a park that's not frequently visited.

Take a deep breath and think of the issues you wish to release. Write them down on the leaves or petals. If you prefer to not write them down, write down a symbol. When you're ready, stand with the wind at your back, holding the petals or leaves. Say:

> *I retain the wisdom of your lesson, but I release you.*
>
> *I release your energy, your hold on me,*
>
> *And all influence you have on me.*
>
> *I no longer need you.*
>
> *I scatter your energy to the winds of the world.*

Release the items one at a time on the wind. Feel the things you wrote down travel on the wind, away from you. These problems are no longer yours. Envision the energy of these items being transformed by the earth. If you wish, use an athame to cut the cord between you and that energy. When you are done, turn and face the wind. Take a deep breath in, inhale the fresh air, and feel the different energy inside of you. Walk away from what you left behind, and do not look back.

Ritual to Summon the Winds of Change

The energy of transformation and change can be called upon anytime you want your magic to happen faster or when you want a non-magical situation to play out. One way to do this is to summon the winds of change, which are also known as the four winds.

This ritual uses the Greek gods of wind, known as the Anemoi, because so much has been written about them. It also starts with the east because that is how most circles are cast. However, you can use different associations and start the ritual facing another direction.

This ritual is particularly exciting to have outside. The winds can blow in and ring wind chimes or play with any other wind toys you might have. If you have it inside, open the windows if possible, or use a fan to stir the air.

MATERIALS
> incense
>
> lighter
>
> besom

Light the incense, take a deep breath of air, and fill your lungs. Exhale, releasing any thoughts or feelings. Hold the besom, face the east, and look into the sky and the air. Read the energy of the air in this direction until you can feel its consciousness. When you feel its awareness of you, call to it:

> *I call upon the East Wind, Eurus,*
> *bringer of rain and warmth.*

Send your energy and power to my ritual.

Hail and welcome!

Turn to the south and sense the energy in the air from that direction. When it seems to come alive, call to it:

I call upon the South Wind, Notus, bringer of heat!

Send your energy and power to my ritual.

Hail and welcome!

Turn to face the west, and once again sense the air and wait to feel a presence.

I call upon the West Wind, Zephyrus,

god of the gentle spring breezes.

Send your energy and power to my ritual.

Hail and welcome!

Face the north and wait to feel a spirit from that direction.

I call upon the North Wind, Boreas, bringer of the cold!

Send your energy and power to my ritual.

Hail and welcome!

Winds of change, I call you today to ask

you to assist me in changing my situation!

Speak about the situation you wish to change. Tell them what needs to be changed and the manner you would like them to change it. These should be tailored to your needs. For example, to bring general positive changes into your life, say something like:

Spirits of the wind, I am ready

for transformations in my life.

I ask you to send good luck, good

experiences, and good people to me.

If you feel creatively blocked, say something like:

Mighty winds!

I call upon you to ask you to remove my creative block.

With your great powers,

let my creative energy flow again!

If you want to catalyze a love magic spell, say something like:

I ask you, O powerful winds who blow over all, to

advance the love magic I cast at the new moon.

Send me a partner in accordance

with the love spell I cast.

With a flicking up motion, sweep the energy around you with the besom. Envision the energy getting lifted into the air. See it get tossed into the winds, and see them taking it and changing it. After the energy has been picked up and transformed, dance with the besom to raise the energy even higher. Try sweeping long circular strokes with the besom, or extend it out as you rotate, or twirl it with your fingers. Embody the energy you wish to have.

When the energy has been raised, stand with your arms outstretched and legs at least hip-distance apart. Say:

Blow, winds of change!

Advance my magic.

Remove my obstacles.

Bring good luck and changes into my life.

May it be so!

Envision your desired outcome and release it to the skies above you. When you feel the message has been received, face the appropriate direction and release them.

North Wind Boreas, West Wind Zephyrus,

South Wind Notus, and East Wind Eurus,

thank you for your assistance. I release you.

Over the next couple of weeks, pay attention when the winds blow. They may be trying to get your attention. Listen to what they have to say.

Magic for Travels

Safe Travels Charm

Travel can be really exciting, but with its constant change, extra communication, and unfamiliar surroundings, it can wear down the brain. You may need an extra boost of air energy to catch your ride on time and have the mental capacity to remember all your belongings. This spell was created to ensure safe travels and a positive presence of mind.

MATERIALS

peppermint oil

smoky quartz crystal about the size of a pinky finger

small piece of aluminum foil or tin foil about the size of two postage stamps

Before leaving on a trip, hold the oil, foil, and the quartz in your hands. Feel their uplifting energy and envision your success throughout your travels. Drop the oil onto the aluminum foil. Roll the foil up and wind it around the middle of the smoky quartz as you say:

Friends of air, I charge you with these tasks:

Give me safe, protected travels.

Bless my travel connections and every place I rest.

Keep my mind sharp and clear.

Let me communicate the right words

to the right people at the right times.

May my travels be a blessing to all.

So mote it be.

Pack the charm in your travel bag or carry-on. Take it with you wherever you go for added protection and luck.

Home is Where I Rest My Head Spell

This spell was developed to take a little bit of home with you wherever your travels might take you. It uses a stuffed animal and many air correspondences.

MATERIALS

mortar and pestle

a pinch or two of dandelion fluff

one small comfrey leaf

a pinch of goldenrod flowers (skip if you're allergic)

two small spoonfuls of dirt from your yard or a potted plant (dried)

a couple of small pieces of clear quartz crystal

pet hair (if applicable)

a small piece of a clean, old t-shirt of a family member cut into tiny pieces (optional)

a large bowl

scissors

a stuffed animal such as a bird or bat

needle and thread

With a mortar and pestle, grind the herbs to a powder. Add a little soil and grind it down with them. Add this mixture to the large bowl along with the crystals, pet hair, and piece of clothing. With scissors, carefully cut a small hole in the stuffed animal somewhere not too noticeable. Pull out the stuffing: place half in the bowl and set half aside. Mix all of the items in the bowl together, cover, and let it sit overnight.

The next day, uncover the bowl and use the mixture to re-stuff the animal. If needed, add the reserved stuffing. Sew up the seam and sleep with your stuffed animal at home before your travels begin. When it's time to go, pack it in your travel bags. Unpack it upon arrival and place it on your travel bed. Hug the stuffed animal whenever you need to feel connected with home again.

Mercury Water Spell for Travel Blessings

On the 15th of May, ancient Romans celebrated Mercuralia for the birth of Mercury. They cut a bay laurel branch, dipped it in the water of a fountain, and sprinkled their heads, merchandise, and ships. Prayers were spoken to Mercury in the hope that he would bless their futures with luck and fortune. Mercury is a knowledgeable traveler, and Mercury Water is a great travel companion. It assists with energies of communication, luck, and power.

MATERIALS

bay laurel leaves

scissors

travel-size spray bottle (i.e. for hairspray)

water from a spring if possible

Cut the bay leaves into long strips and slide them into the spray bottle. As you pour the water, say:

I call upon swift-footed Mercury, messenger of the gods.

I ask you to guide me in my travels

with luck, fortune, and wisdom!

Shake the bottle and place it in sunshine for an hour. Before leaving for your trip, lightly spray yourself, your luggage, your vehicle, and anything else that's going with you. Pack the water with you and use it when you arrive. As you spray the water, say:

Mercury, I call upon thee.

I ask for your blessings in all you see!

Spirit Magic

Spell to Attract a Sylph

As the smallest of air spirits, sylphs have a light, effervescent energy. They're quite friendly, and they like nothing more than to play, be seen, and help. This spell uses bubbles to attract them and gives you the option to work with them in other ways.

MATERIALS

>   bubbles
>
>   outdoors

To befriend a sylph, go outdoors. Let your expression be light, airy, and friendly. Channel the element of air in your demeanor. Begin to blow bubbles with your magical breath by focusing on the element of air as you exhale. Between rewetting the bubble wand, and blowing more bubbles, say:

Come to me, sylphs, spirits of the air!

I blow these bubbles for your play!

When you feel the presence of a light spirit nearby, encourage it to play with the bubbles until you see them do strange things, like being tossed in a whirlwind or being still at one point without moving. You can continue to blow bubbles for them, which will likely be a fun experience. Or, you can also ask a sylph to work for you. Ask it to perform a simple task for you in reward for a treat later. For example:

> *If you tell Andre I'm bringing chocolate cake to the*
> *party, I'll light some incense for you later.*

Sylphs can do light weather magic, relay messages, aid with light intellectual matters, and give you creative energy. If you're having trouble invoking one, you may also play music or burn incense to attract one. If the wind whips up too much or you start to feel dizzy, thank them and say goodbye.

Spell to Connect with the Spirit of a Bird

Birds are fascinating creatures. We rarely get to commune with many of them, though. If you work with a particular bird in your magic, you can get in touch with their energy. This practice calls upon the collective spirit of a certain kind of bird by using their feather. This is likely the best magic for working with birds unless you're extremely familiar with a specific bird, and you feel they would allow you to connect with them.

MATERIALS
a feather

Hold the feather in your hands, and begin to slow your breaths. Notice all of the features of the feather—the colors, the patterns (if any), and other physical qualities of it. Attune your energy to the bird's. Envision the bird is before you and make a slow bow to it. Say its common name three times, then say: "What message have you for me?" Listen for the answer and thank it.

Ritual to Summon a Spirit

Several cultures believe that spirits imbibe our offerings. Air energy, in the form of burning incense, is an excellent offering to call upon spirits. You may wish to summon your beloved dead, a familiar, a muse, a guardian spirit, or any other spirit you may wish to communicate with.

Although you don't need to have a summoning ritual to speak with spirits, this process formalizes meeting a new spirit, ensuring protection from baneful or chaotic spirits. This summoning spell can also conjure a spirit to you that has not responded when you called previously in a more casual way.

Offering incense can be a practice in and of itself, or it can be incorporated into part of a larger ritual. You could do this anytime, but it would be especially beneficial during Samhain season, when the veil between the worlds is thinner. The herbs in this incense facilitate communication with all kinds of spirits. If you can't burn incense, use mister spray bottles with a combination of essential oils and strongly brewed tea.

MATERIALS

> private space
>
> at least thirty minutes
>
> a black candle (any size)
>
> Samhain incense from Chapter 12
>
> mortar and pestle
>
> a charcoal disk
>
> incense holder

a lighter or matches

divination tool such as tarot

Book of Shadows

writing tool

Cleanse your ritual area with burning herbs or your preferred method. Cast a circle around you for protection. To ensure safety with spirits, call upon the Elemental Guardians of Air or use a protective phrase, for example:

I summon my guardian spirits to
keep unwanted spirits out.
No spirit shall enter this circle other than those who
have my highest good in mind (or those I summon).

Light the candle. Breathe deeply, and let each breath cleanse your mind of thoughts until you are like a clear vessel filled with air. Allow yourself to slip into a light trance state of mind. Mix the incense, using your intuition to know how much to add of each ingredient.

Grind the incense together with a mortar and pestle. Inhale deeply of the mixture, and allow its aromas to take your thoughts away. As you grind, recite your intention for the incense's purpose in the summoning. For example:

Open my mind to communicate with spirits.

Be more specific if you wish. Repeat the intention several times as you slip deeper and deeper into a trance state. Let your energy align with your words and the herbs until you feel you are one.

Light the incense charcoal. Let it burn for a couple of minutes while meditating. When the disk is ready, add a pinch of the incense and call your magic back to you. Call upon the incense to do the work you programmed it with. You can do this by focusing on it or sending it a nudge of your energy. Let it react to your command and come alive. You may experience this sensation by hearing the spell you spoke as it burns, or you may feel the energy rise with the smoke as it burns. If you're more of a visual person, you might see the energy in the incense.

Waft the incense toward you and inhale the fragrance of the burning herbs. Let the aromas saturate your mind, and make any last energetic shifts to get into the otherworldly state of mind.

With a clear, strong voice, summon a spirit by speaking the name or purpose of the spirit and an invocation to them. Speak your words into the incense—let your words combine and rise with the smoke. For example:

> *I call upon the spirit of Laurie Demarco, my beloved*
> *deceased aunt. Laurie, I call upon your spirit and ask*
> *you to be with me. I offer this incense to you. Come, assist*
> *me in my magical work to bless and protect this home.*

Or:

> *I call upon a spirit who is interested in becoming my*
> *familiar. Come to me and make your presence known.*

When you're aware of the presence of a spirit, ask them to speak to you. Listen with your second hearing for their voice. It might sound like your thoughts, but with a different accent or voice. Listen to what they have to say. Ask them questions about anything, including the future, your present, or the past. You could ask for gifts or insights. You could even ask about other worlds.

Once you hear their message, write it down into your Book of Shadows so you don't forget it. You may want to use tarot cards, a pendulum, or some other form of divination to discern the message. You could also try your hand at automatic writing with the spirit, or attempt an out-of-body experience. If you're meeting your familiar for the first time, hold off on any big magical acts until trust has been developed between you, preferably over several sessions. Add additional incense to the charcoal every few minutes. This keeps your mindset otherworldly and it also continues to feed the spirits.

When you're finished speaking with a spirit, thank them and bid them farewell. As soon as you feel that they're gone, take a breath or two to pause. If you wish, you can clear the circle by sending a burst of flaming blue or violet energy out from your chest until you feel the circle is cleared. This removes any remaining energy that is not yours. However, it expends energy, so do it sparingly if you have low energy or if you're new to the general technique. Call upon other spirits if you wish.

When you're done with the ritual, thank your guardian spirits and release the circle. Ground back into your body by eating some food and drinking water. Spirit work takes a lot of energy and can be very draining for some people. Being aware of this protects you from an energetic hangover and feeling wiped out.

If you have good benefits from this practice, use the same incense whenever you call upon these spirits. Keep tabs on what you used and how successful they were in assisting you. Change the recipe to refine it according to your needs. You may want to use this incense and method to keep in touch with them on a regular basis.

Automatic Writing Ritual to Communicate with a Spirit

Automatic writing is an ancient method of entering a trance to communicate with spirits while writing down their words. The trance state shuts down the cerebral cortex, the part of the brain responsible for thinking and language. With an empty mind, the automatic writer lets the writing tool move of its own accord, or asks questions and receives answers.

MATERIALS

Book of Shadows or paper

a pen that flows easily over the paper but does not allow ink to leak out if it's not moving

a darkened room

a candle (any size or shape)

a lighter or matches.

Choose a time and place where you won't be disturbed for a couple of hours. Cleanse your space, cast a protective circle, and call upon your guardian spirits. Light the candle.

I light this candle and summon a helpful spirit who has

only my best interests in mind. Be with me now. Spirit,

I ask that you assist me with automatic writing

and reveal the secrets of the world to me.

Clear your mind. Take a deep breath, then empty your lungs. Repeat. On the next inhalation, breathe in the energy of air and spirit. Let this feeling saturate your mind and body. See it as an energy that encompasses you. Continue to breathe deeply and rhythmically, following whatever pattern takes you into a trance state of mind.

When you feel ready, pick up the writing tool and hold it so that it touches the paper. Hold the paper with your other hand. Position yourself so that you are in a comfortable writing position. Breathe in the energy of air and spirit again. Let yourself go in this expansive energy. Let the pen start to move in your hand.

If this is your first time attempting automatic writing, let your hand go while your mind wanders. Try to really enjoy this feeling and just explore what comes. Once you feel proficient in this, ask questions—ask what is meant by certain phrases, who the spirit is, why something is happening in your life, and so on. The questions can be spoken out loud or written down. Continue writing as you receive the answers from the spirit. This is a more advanced technique that requires a mental shift between the conscious state to the trance state.

Once you are satisfied with the experience, place the pen down. Thank and release the spirit. Release any additional guardian spirits and open the circle. Ground back into your body by stretching and moving around. You may wish to eat and drink something as well. Be sure to review what you wrote and rewrite it if the handwriting was messy. The sooner this can happen, the better chance you have of getting it correct.

Chapter 12

HOLIDAYS AND THE AIR WHEEL OF THE YEAR

Air is all around us, and yet, it's the one element we can't see. Similarly, the element of air is just as pervasive in many aspects of our lives, though not always evident. When we choose to celebrate those special times when air is most prominent, we create more space for the element of air. This can increase our understanding of our own mental processes, spirituality, changes, communications, and several other air aspects.

Moments to Celebrate Air

Youth

Air corresponds with the youthful parts of life, from birth to puberty. As babies, our first breath marks the beginning of our lives. Children embody the active, changeable, and expansive aspects of the element of air. Our childhoods are days when we imagine, learn something new every day, and explore the world around us. It's also when we learn how to talk, write, and express ourselves. Some also have their first spiritual experiences in their youth. Hermes, one of the deities most associated with nearly every facet of air, is described as a youth.

Celebration of the New Year

Although many Witches celebrate Samhain or Yule as the new year, the calendar year starts on January 1, and the first new year celebrations were definitely pagan. The Greek deity Janus was honored the whole month, but especially on the first. The custom of kissing your beloved under hanging mistletoe is Druidic in origin, and drinking alcohol on this day is a Roman tradition. The beginning of the year is an especially airy time of fresh starts and declarations of change. It's a time when many people write out their intentions for the year in the form of resolutions. This combines the powers of the changed year and the spoken or written word.

Springtime

Springtime is the designated season associated with air. It's a time when fresh life buds, colorful flowers appear, and blustery winds blow their aromas far and wide. There's a feeling of fresh starts and newness in the air. Springtime is the season when Persephone leaves the underworld and returns to our world. The Roman goddess Flora was also honored at this time with the festival Floralia, which occurred during the last days of April and the first days of May.

Springtime gives us the opportunity to ponder the significance of the seasons with the current changes in our lives, from cold winter into the warmer part of the year. Celebrate springtime by cutting flowers, eating fruit and nourishing foods, and planting seeds. It's also a great time to work magic for new beginnings, hope, rebirth, fertility, growth, and purification.

Back to School Time

Where I live, most of the kids and university students return to school in the fall after a summer break. Not only is this an intensive learning period, but it's also the start of the school year. I remember it as a momentous time, especially as a child. I usually had so much freedom that summer to do what I wanted that I didn't even mind going back. I remember the excitement of new clothes, new school supplies, and the feeling that anything could happen. The first few days especially were full of changes and discussing ideas. I may have romanticized this, but there's definitely beauty about a fresh start.

Graduation Ceremonies

At the end of years of school, loads of tests, and the refining of intellect comes a time to celebrate one's accomplishments. Graduation ceremonies are pivotal moments of change and possibility. They usually have many speeches and celebrate intellectual accomplishments, including recognizing the valedictorian. Graduation hats are of particular air significance—not only did they represent intelligence, but they were traditionally red to signify blood. Even the act of throwing one's hat into the air symbolizes the change that graduation brings—the end of one phase of life and the beginning of another.

Spiritual Initiation Ceremonies

Just as school graduations celebrate the accomplishment of the mind, spiritual initiations celebrate the achievements of the spirit. These liminal experiences are often the start of a new chapter in our magical lives.

Moving

There comes a time for most people when we have to go from one home to another. The act of moving can be such a big change, especially if it's to another city. Virtually everything is new, and it's imperative to learn the locations of necessary places like groceries and transportation routes. These days, many Witches use burning herbs or incense to cleanse, promote protection, and remove stagnant energy in their new spaces.

Death

One of the biggest changes we'll ever experience is the one that comes about right at the end of our lives—dying. Even experiencing the death of a loved one can bring about such a big change that it can feel like the world is different. The presence of spirits and departed loved ones connects us even more to the element of air during these times.

Air and the Wheel of the Year

The days on the wheel of the year mark important times for the sun and the earth. They give us reasons to celebrate and reflect on where we are, where we've been, and where we're going. If you have a ritual on these days or observe them in any way, it's likely that air will be a part of it.

The ideas in this section give you a way of looking at the element of air throughout the year. They can be used in ritual on that day, or you could also use them any time during the days leading up to the holiday or afterward, observing the season of the holiday, for example, the Yuletide season.

This section has recipes for incense, teas, and simmer pots that were inspired by the wheel of the year. An abundance of ingredients were suggested for these recipes—feel free to adapt them if you don't have all of the items. The most evocative ingredients of each season were chosen for the sabbat incenses, including many air-corresponding herbs. To blend the incense, mix the ingredients together in fairly even proportions unless otherwise mentioned. A small pinch of each ingredient is likely all you'll need for a charcoal disk. Grind the incense with a mortar and pestle until they're homogenous. If you choose to use essential oils or a sticky resin like pine sap, skip the mortar and pestle, and add them directly onto the burning charcoal instead of mixing them with the other ingredients. This will keep your mortar and pestle clean.

The teas in this section were chosen among the list of corresponding herbs that represent the element of air. Combine them in fairly even proportions unless otherwise mentioned. Use about a tablespoon per cup of tea, or adjust to taste. Steep 3 to 5 minutes. The teas for the warmer months can be brewed and chilled ahead of time for a refreshing, seasonal drink.

Simmer pots are a wonderful way to use herbs and create a little kitchen witchery. Not only do they emit fantastic aromas, but they also have the added benefit of humidifying the air, which is especially nice during the dry winter days. To make a simmer pot, toss the ingredients into a small saucepan on the back of the stove. Add water until the pot is about ¾ full. Boil gently for five minutes, and then set the heat to simmer. Enjoy the aromas as they waft through your kitchen. Add water about twice an hour or whenever it's low. A crockpot may be substituted for simmer pots.

Yule or Winter Solstice

This winter holiday sabbat marks the shortest day of the year and celebrates the rebirth of the sun. It's a time when the cool air is perfumed with the jolly scent of pines, spiced apple cider, cool peppermint candy, and warm fruitcake. Holiday music and bells fill the air, making things feel a little brighter despite the long, dark nights. This time of the year is associated with Odin leading the Wild Hunt across the skies.

When you call upon air in your Yule ritual, bring to mind the cold snap of the air, the holiday aromas, the sound of bells, the energy of the rebirthed sun, and the dawning of a new solar year.

Yuletide Incense

Frankincense, myrrh, sage, juniper berries, bay leaves, cinnamon (crushed sticks or powder), clove, and pine or spruce (fragrant needles or resin), a half a part of mace powder, and orange oil.

Yuletide Simmer Pot

A five-inch long cinnamon stick, one tablespoon of cloves, one six-inch clipping of pine needles, five bay leaves, one teaspoon orange peel, one teaspoon powdered nutmeg.

Imbolc

Imbolc celebrates the return of the light. By that time, it's clear that the days are growing longer. In many parts of the hemisphere, the earth is still cold, and there's little to do outside besides travel from one warm place to another. This is why many people associate Imbolc with the hearth. It's the perfect time of the year to hang out in the kitchen, make spiced cookies and savory stews, light candles, and feast with loved ones. Imbolc is all about creating warmth where there is none and trusting that the wheel of the year will turn again. This holiday helps us think bright, beautiful thoughts about the sunny months to come. Traditionally, this holiday also celebrates Brigid, the Irish goddess of fire, healing, poetry, fertility, and metal-smithing, among other things. It's also a great time for performing a home cleansing ritual by sweeping your home with a besom.

When you invoke the element of air at Imbolc, bring to mind all of the new beginnings, change, light, and transformations occurring. Think of the chilly air outside and the smell of snow and ice. You could also call upon fixed Aquarian energy for its innovative spirit, which can help get you through the coldest of times.

Imbolc Incense

Black peppercorns, allspice powder, cinnamon powder, ginger powder, clove powder, portion of a vanilla bean, crushed bay leaves, white copal.

Imbolc Simmer Pot

Half a tablespoon of allspice powder, a five-inch cinnamon stick, a tablespoon of ginger powder, a tablespoon of cloves, half a vanilla bean (or one teaspoon of vanilla extract), half a tablespoon of nutmeg, and two bay leaves.

Ostara or Spring Equinox

At this time of the year, when the days and nights are of equal length, the air smells of wet earth, melting snow, and early spring flowers such as croci, snowdrops, possibly even daffodils. Birds collect grass to make new nests to hold their eggs. Spring is arriving, change is in the air, and everything seems new and full of hope.

These Ostara recipes evoke a fresh green aroma with the earthy smell of roots. The tea tastes fresh and cleansing—green tea and lemongrass lift the spirits, while the dandelion, marshmallow, and valerian roots imbue it with an earthy flavor that's perfectly balanced, just like the equinox.

When you invoke the element of air at the equinox, use the energy of balance, the aromas of the spring flowers, and the sound of birds. Bring to mind the mentality of hope and change.

Spring Equinox Incense

Clover blossoms, dandelion root, marshmallow root, lemongrass, tiny bit of valerian root, sweetgrass.

Spring Equinox Tea

Green tea, clover blossoms, dandelion root, marshmallow root, lemongrass, horsetail, and a tiny bit of valerian root.

Beltane

At this beautiful sabbat, the air is fresh and fragrant with the scents of flowers bursting into bloom nearly everywhere. Springtime has definitely arrived, which is evident in the bees buzzing around, and birds that have chirping little chicks in their nests. This time is associated with psychic ability, spirits, and creativity, when many people believe the veil between the worlds is thinner.

When you call upon the element of air in your Beltane rituals, invoke the scent of flowers in bloom and the mentality of pleasure and love.

Beltane Incense

Jasmine flowers or oil, vervain, chamomile flowers, damiana leaves, ylang ylang oil, and neroli oil.

BELTANE TEA

Lavender flowers, hibiscus flowers, rose petals, red clover, jasmine flowers, chamomile flowers, and damiana leaves.

Litha or Midsummer

Midsummer is the time of the year when the days are at their longest. The crops are strong and hardy by now, and the sun's light can be enjoyed late into the night. The herbaceous aromas of the magical midsummer incense and tea have the power to lift the spirits and bring the energy of the sun to the senses. They're especially wonderful if you harvest any of the ingredients from your own garden.

When you call upon the element of air for your midsummer or Litha ritual, invoke the spirit of the sun at its peak, the green man or the green one, the green aroma of crops and herbs, and the mentality of strength and fertility. Invoke Gemini's warm, glib banter and the mutable aspects of the summer season that adapts to our intentions.

MAGICAL MIDSUMMER INCENSE

Lemongrass, thyme, rosemary, lavender leaves or flowers, catnip, parsley, sage, mint, and hops.

MAGICAL MIDSUMMER TEA

Witch hazel, green sage, thyme, catnip, clover blossoms, yarrow flowers, hops, peppermint, and a pinch of rosemary.

Lughnasadh or Lammas

At the time of Lughnasadh, the harvest is bountiful. Flowers still scent the air, but there's more of a maturity, which can be seen in the tall crops and plants. The amount of sunlight is decreasing, but the heat is usually more intense. This is traditionally the time of the year when the first fields of grain are harvested and bread is made. The sweet sound of birds and insects fills the air, making the days and nights feel cozy and calm.

When you call upon the element of air at Lughnasadh, think about reaping the rewards from the work you've done, the sweet smell of baking bread, and the music of the natural world.

Lughnasadh Harvest Incense

Frankincense, angelica root, dragon's blood, yarrow flowers, vervain, rosemary, and half a portion of ginger.

Lughnasadh Harvest Tea

Yarrow flowers, gotu kola, horsetail, vervain, eleuthero ginseng, rosemary, and half a portion of dried lemon peel.

Mabon or Autumn Equinox

The autumn equinox marks a change in the warm summer days. The nights fall sooner, and some nights might have a chill in the air. In the far northern latitudes, the leaves start to turn colors. Mabon is the second harvest, when many fruits and vegetables are harvested. It's the time of equal days and equal nights. The moment after equinox is exact, cooler, darker times rule, marking six months of inward journeying. It's a time of storing up for the winter and getting the land and our minds ready for what's to come.

When you call upon air at the autumn equinox, invoke the balance between light and dark, and the aromas of apples, squash, tomatoes, and herbs. Bring forth Libra's values of justice and fairness, and use the cardinal energy to create peace and love that will last throughout the long winter.

AUTUMN EQUINOX INCENSE

Sandalwood (chips or powder), cinnamon, myrrh, cloves, cardamom, ylang ylang oil, and a tiny bit of vetivert (plant or oil).

AUTUMN EQUINOX TEA

Double portion of black tea, dried orange peel, crushed cinnamon sticks, half a portion of cloves, cardamom pods (broken open), and ginger.

Samhain

At this time of the year, dried leaves crackle underfoot and the air often has a cold snap. Perhaps you can sense the thinning of the veil and how thick the air is with spirits. Samhain is the third harvest, when the garden and crops are no more. Traditionally, this was the time of livestock culling.

When you call upon the element of air at Samhain, call upon the spirits of the ancestors, wisdom, change, and the scent of compost.

SAMHAIN INCENSE

Mugwort, nutmeg powder or essential oil, fennel, thyme, angelica root, eyebright, and vervain.

SAMHAIN SIMMER POT

One teaspoon nutmeg powder, one anise star, one sliced apple, one five-inch cinnamon stick, one tablespoon cloves, and half a tablespoon allspice powder.

Days of the Week

The days of the week have many associations and corresponding deities and actions. However, they could be viewed from an air perspective regarding magical workings. The information in this section relates to the air-corresponding parts of the days only.

- Monday is associated with Selene, Hekate, and spirits. It's a good time to gain greater control over emotions and meditate. You could also try astral projection, necromancy, and divination. Magic for change is favored on this day as well.

- Tuesday is the day for Mars. Even though Mars is not an air deity, this is still a good day to take action on something you've been meaning to do for a while. The energy of this day can be used for magic for justice, purification, and seeking the truth.

- Wednesday is associated with Mercury, Hermes, Athena, and Odin. The best air magic for this day includes taking action, communication, conducting business, getting creative, travel, and using your intelligence.

- Thursday is connected with Thor, Juno, Jupiter, and Zeus. Use the expansive power of this day in your magic for abundance, justice, freedom, power, leadership, and success.

- Friday is ruled by Frigg. It's a great time to work magic for communications, especially with loved ones. It can also be used to purify the mind and bring about greater wisdom.

- Saturday is associated with Saturn and Hekate. As the work week transitions into the weekend, use the energy to make changes, cleanse, bind, banish, and to create greater freedom and self-discipline.

- Sunday is the day of the Sun and solar deities such as Helios, Ra, and Mithras. Use the magical energy of this day to start new projects (especially at sunrise), take action, be creative, build abundance, and seek visions. Other magical work blessed on this day include justice work, leadership, fame, and refining the power of the mind.

Seize the Day

There are countless days when we have a chance to reflect upon the element of air in our lives. Our accomplishments and the turning of the seasons mirror our own internal changes as well as the changes in the world. Use these times to cultivate a flexible and adaptable mind that embraces all the gifts of the present moment.

Conclusion

ANY WAY THE WIND BLOWS

Mastery of the element of air requires us to embody its many aspects. We must become the arbitrators of change in our own lives. We must venture out into the unknown realms of air and return with more knowledge. We must be able to focus, communicate, take action, and adapt to a constantly changing world. Fortunately, the element of air rewards those who desire "to know." It reveals its secrets to those who seek them.

Of course, no element exists in a vacuum. Balance among the four elements is essential. Their energies together create the dynamic of life—mind, body, and spirit. When these elements are in harmony, we can truly thrive. While I personally adore the element of air, I'm looking forward to developing a closer relationship with the other elements. I hope you too will seek out their perspectives, energies, and wisdom as well.

I'd like to leave you with an airy blessing. My wish for you is this: every time you look up at the sky above, may you receive all the blessings of an empowered association with the element of air. May the sky remind you of the most poignant lessons in this book. These will inevitably be different for everyone—for some, the sky will remind them to breathe and expand their energy. For others, they'll remember to exercise discernment and logic more often. Perhaps it will inspire you to feel the spirits in the wind or transmit your wishes through the magical realm of air.

Whatever your personal lesson is, I hope it gives you wings and perspective. Thank you so much for taking this flight with me.

Sincerely,
Astrea

ACKNOWLEDGMENTS

FIRST AND FOREMOST, I thank my husband Tim for our great love, for keeping me grounded, for always finding my glasses, and for inspiring me with his creative work ethic. Next, a big thanks to Scarlett, Ashes, Andrea, Kari, and Christine for our inspiring conversations and amazingly supportive friendships. I also thank my mom, sister, and other family members for their continued support and love.

Special thanks go to my Llewellyn editor Heather Greene, who makes my books better with her clever insights. I'm lucky to work with such an organized and smart person. Thanks also to the other helpful people at Llewellyn—having someone believe in my work is invaluable.

Thanks to all my fabulous writing friends at Patheos Pagan who are so supportive and helped lift my voice, especially Jason Mankey, Brianne Ravenwolf, Mat Auryn, Cyndi Brannen, Phoenix LeFae, Gwion Raven, Laura Tempest Zakroff, Kelden, Lilith Dorsey, Devin Hunter, Lisa Bland, Elliot Director, Gwyn, Misha Magdalene, and Irisanya Moon. Thanks to others in the community as well, particularly Meg Rosenbriar, Louisa Blackthorn, Lisa Marie Basile, Luna Crowley, Briony Silver, Chris Forester, Steven Intermill, Car, Ode, Jacki Smith, Mika Hills, Mabh Savage, Alfred

Willowhawk, Kendra McMahan, Carly Rose, Jennifer Williams, Tam and Dale Rois, Debbie Lewis, and Luna Eclipse.

Thanks to my other wonderful friends Rhiannon, Mary, Laura, Seth, Tatiara, Ali, Stefanie, Penny, Heather, Amy, Joe, Mere, Haley, Shay, Vida, Keri, Theresa, Joelle, Dorian, Fenix, Jesica, Irish, Colleen, Gabriel, Kerrie, Chris, Shari, Lissa, Leslie, and Tammy. Thanks to everyone at the Intuitive Witchcraft facebook group too—you are all amazing.

Thanks to Maria and my other friends at Baba Yaga's Hut. Thanks to Selena Fox, Circle Sanctuary, and everyone at the Pagan Spirit Gathering who have inspired me over the years, especially Susu and Penny Goody for teaching wondrous workshops on weather witchery.

Thanks to my local writing group and fans of my fiction, who walked through *The House of Transformation* and rallied for *Belle Dame Sans Merci*. Lastly, I thank Casper and Crow for continued inspiration and guidance.

Appendix

AIR CORRESPONDENCE CHART

Keywords	The mind, imagination, thoughts, communication, spirit, change, expansion
Direction	East (or North)
Season	Spring (or Winter)
Time of Day	Dawn (or Night)
Astrological Signs	Gemini, Libra, Aquarius
Planets	Mercury, Jupiter, Uranus
Tarot	Swords, The Fool, The Emperor, Justice, Judgment
Chakra	Throat, third eye, crown
Tools	Sword/athame, censer, bell, and sometimes wand
Incense	Cedar, copal, frankincense, myrrh, sandalwood

Elementals	Sylphs
Colors	Yellow, white, sky blue, purple
Gems	Amethyst, charoite, fluorite, lapis lazuli, moldavite, quartz, sodalite
Plants	Aster, dandelion, lavender, mint, parsley, rosemary, sage, thyme, vervain
Trees	Aspen, bay laurel, elder, fir, hawthorn, hazel, linden, maple, oak, walnut, witch hazel, yew
Natural Objects	Feathers, insect wings, smoke
Animals	All birds, bats, and flying insects such as butterflies, moths, dragonflies, crickets, bees
Deity	Athena, Au Set, Ayida Wedo, Hermes, Horus, Inanna, Jupiter, Obatalá, Odin, Oyá, Uranus, Zeus
Sense	Smell, sound
Magical Lesson	To know

BIBLIOGRAPHY

Adler, Margot. *Drawing Down the Moon: Witches, Druids, Goddess-Worshippers, and Other Pagans in America.* Revised Ed. New York: Penguin Books, 2006.

Agrippa, Heinrich Cornelius. "Occult Philosophy Book 1: Natural Magic." Joseph H. Peterson, 2000. Accessed November 24, 2019. http://www.esotericarchives.com/agrippa/agrippa1.htm#chap3

Agrippa, Heinrich Cornelius. "Occult Philosophy Book 3: Ceremonial Magic." Joseph H. Peterson, 2000. Accessed November 24, 2019. http://www.esotericarchives.com/agrippa/agripp3b.htm.

All Nursery Rhymes. "One for Sorrow." Accessed November 27, 2019. https://allnurseryrhymes.com/one-for-sorrow/.

Alvarado, Denise. *The Voodoo Hoodoo Spellbook.* San Francisco: Weiser Books, 2011.

Attar, Farid Ud-Din. *Conference of the Birds.* Translated by Afkham Darbandi and Dick Davis. London: Penguin Classics, 1984.

Alexander, Skye. *Modern Guide to Witchcraft: Your Complete Guide to Witches, Covens, & Spells.* Avon: Adams Media, 2014.

Apuleius. *The Golden Ass Or, A Book of Changes.* Translated by Joel Relihan. Indianapolis: Hackett Publishing Company, 2007.

Baribeau, Renee. *Winds of Spirit: Ancient Wisdom Tools for Navigating Relationships, Health, and the Divine.* New York: Hay House, 2018.

Bauer, Susan Wise. *The Story of the World: History for the Classical Child. Volume 2: The Middle Ages From the Fall of Rome to the Rise of the Renaissance.* Second Edition. Charles City: Peace Hill Press, 2007.

Basile, Lisa Marie. *Light Magic for Dark Times: More Than 100 Spells, Rituals, and Practices for Coping in a Crisis.* Beverly: Fair Winds Press, 2018.

Basile, Lisa Marie. *Magical Writing Grimoire: Use the Word as Your Wand for Magic, Manifestation &Ritual.* Beverly: Fair Winds Press, 2020.

BBC News. "Fairy Tale Origins Thousands of Years Old, Researchers Say." Published January 20, 2016. Accessed March 21, 2020. https://www.bbc.com/news/uk-35358487.

Blake, Deborah. *The Witch's Broom: The Craft, Lore, and Magick of Broomsticks.* Woodbury: Llewellyn Publications, 2014.

Blakely, Sandra. *Myth, Ritual and Metallurgy in Ancient Greece and Recent Africa.* Oxford: Cambridge University Press, 2006.

Borges, Jorge Luis. *The Book of Imaginary Beings.* Translated by Andrew Hurley. New York: Penguin Group, 2005.

Brand, John, and Henry Bourne. *Observations on Popular Antiquities.* London: J. Johnson, 1777.

Brown, Ann. "How Many Breaths Do You Take Each Day?" The EPA Blog. Published April 24, 2014. Accessed 7/3/2019. https://blog.epa.gov/2014/04/28/how-many-breaths-do-you -take-each-day/.

Campbell, Polly. "Movement Can Help You Feel Better—Fast." *Psychology Today.* Posted January 23, 2013. Accessed December 11, 2019. https://www.psychologytoday.com/us/blog/imperfect -spirituality/201301/movement-can-help-you-feel-better-fast.

Chevallier, Andrew. *Herbal Remedies (Eyewitness Companions)*. New York: DK Publishing, 2007.

Cunningham, Scott. *Cunningham's Encyclopedia of Crystal, Gem, and Metal Magic*. Second Edition. Woodbury: Llewellyn Worldwide, 2018.

Cunningham, Scott. *Wicca: A Guide for the Solitary Practitioner*. First Edition, revised. Woodbury: Llewellyn Worldwide, 2004.

Daimler, Morgan. *Fairies: A Guide to the Celtic Fair Folk*. Alresford: John Hunt Publishing, 2017.

Davies, Owen. "The Rise of Modern Magic." In *The Oxford Illustrated History of Witchcraft & Magic*, edited by Owen Davies, 167–194. Oxford: Oxford University Press, 2017.

De Blécourt, Willem. "Witches on Screen." In *The Oxford Illustrated History of Witchcraft & Magic*, edited by Owen Davies, 253-280. Oxford: Oxford University Press, 2017.

Dell, Christopher. *The Occult, Witchcraft & Magic: An Illustrated History*. London: Thames & Hudson, 2016.

Dias, Brian G. and Kerry J. Ressler. *Parental Olfactory Experience Influences Behavior and Neural Structure in Subsequent Generations*. Nature.com. Published December 1, 2013. Accessed December 28, 2019. https://www.nature.com/articles/nn.3594.

Dictionary.com. "Neopaganism." Accessed December 21, 2019. https://www.dictionary.com/browse/neopaganism.

Dubats, Sally. *Natural Magick: The Essential Witch's Grimoire*. New York: Citadel Press, 2002.

Emba, Christine. "An Entire Generation is Losing Hope. Enter the Witch." *Washington Post*, published November 13, 2018, accessed December 28, 2019. https://www.washingtonpost.com/opinions /an-entire-generation-is-losing-hope-enter-the-witch/2018/11 /13/a939001e-e6c9-11e8-bbdb-72fdbf9d4fed_story.html.

Encounters With the Good People. "Encounters with the Good People." Last modified December 10, 2019, accessed January 2, 2020. https://encounterswiththegoodpeople.com/index.php /category/story/.

Faerywolf, Storm. *Betwixt and Between: Exploring the Faery Tradition of Witchcraft.* Woodbury: Llewellyn Publications, 2017.

Filan, Kenos. *The Haitian Voodoo Handbook: Protocols for Riding with the Lwa.* Rochester: Destiny Books, 2007.

Frazier, Sir James. *The Golden Bough: A Study in Magic and Religion.* Abridged ed. New York: Macmillan, 1922, Bartelby.com, 2000. Published 2000, accessed September 9, 2019. https://www .bartleby.com/196/13.html.

Garrett, Lynn. "Season of the Witch: Mind Body Spirit Books." *Publishers Weekly.* Published August 2, 2019. Accessed December 28, 2019. https://www.publishersweekly.com/pw/by-topic/new -titles/adult-announcements/article/80847-season-of-the-witch -mind-body-spirit-books.html.

Godfinder. "Symbolism and Natural History of the Sacred Trees." Accessed April 5, 2020. http://www.godfinder.org/sacred-tree .html.

Grasse, Ray. *The Waking Dream: Unlocking the Symbolic Language of Our Lives.* Wheaton: Quest Books, 1996.

Greene, Heather. *Bell, Book, and Camera: A Critical History of Witches in American Film and Television.* Jefferson: McFarland & Company, 2018.

Greer, John Michael. *The Occult Book: A Chronological Journey from Alchemy to Wicca.* New York: Sterling, 2017.

Grimassi, Raven. "The Craft of the Witches." Llewellyn. Published September 1, 2002. Accessed April 28, 2020. https://www .llewellyn.com/journal/article/423.

Grimassi, Raven. *What We Knew in the Night: Reawakening the Heart of Witchcraft.* Newburyport: Red Wheel, 2019.

Grundy, Benjamin. "New Study Confirms Maori Legend of Giant Eagle." Mysterious Universe. Published September 15, 2009. Accessed November 25, 2019. https://mysteriousuniverse .org/2009/09/new-study-confirms-maori-legend-of-giant-eagle/.

Guggenheim, Bill and Judy. *Hello From Heaven: A New Field of Research—After-Death-Communication—Confirms that Life and Love are Eternal.* New York: Bantam, 1997.

Hall, Judy. *Principles of Psychic Protection.* New York: Thorsons, 1999.

Hamer, Ashley. "Here's Why Smells Trigger Such Vivid Memories." Curiosity.com. Published January 31, 2018.Accessed December 28, 2019. https://curiosity.com/topics/heres-why-smells-trigger -such-vivid-memories-curiosity/.

Hamilton, Edith. *Mythology: Timeless Tales of Gods and Heroes.* New York: Mentor Books, 1940.

Hamilton, Virginia. *In the Beginning: Creation Stories from Around the World.* New York: Harcourt, Inc., 1988.

Handwerk, Brian. "From St. Nicholas to Santa Claus: The Surprising Origins of Kris Kringle." *National Geographic.* Published December 25, 2018. Accessed October 23, 2019.https://www .nationalgeographic.com/news/2018/12/131219-santa-claus -origin-history-christmas-facts-st-nicholas/.

Harlowe, George E., and Anna S. Sofianides. *Gems and Crystals From One of the World's Greatest Collections.* New York: Sterling Signature, 2015.

Theoi. "Harpyiai." Theoi.com. Accessed April 20, 2020. https://www.theoi.com/Pontios/Harpyiai.html.

Hewitt, J.F. *History and Chronology of the Myth-Making Age.* London: J. Parker and Co., 1901.

Hopman, Ellen Evert. *A Druid's Herbal for the Sacred Earth Year.* New York: Simon and Schuster, 1994.

Hull, Emily. "Graduation Ceremony Traditions and History." *CNY News*, June 19, 2013. Accessed May 8, 2020. https://cnynews.com/graduation-ceremony-traditions-and-history/.

Hunter, Devin. *The Witch's Book of Spirits.* Woodbury: Llewellyn Publications, 2017.

IPCC (Intergovernmental Panel on Climate Change). *Climate Change 2014: Synthesis Report. Contribution of Working Groups I, II and III to the Fifth Assessment Report of the Intergovernmental Panel on Climate Change* [Core Writing Team, R.K. Pachauri and L.A. Meyer (eds.)]. IPCC, Geneva, Switzerland, 151 pp., 2014.

Jones, David E. *An Instinct for Dragons.* Milton Park: Routledge, 2016.

Kelden. *The Crooked Path: An Introduction to Traditional Witchcraft.* Woodbury: Llewellyn Publications, 2020.

Kinkele, Thomas. *Incense and Incense Rituals.* Twin Lakes: Lotus Press, 2005.

Koehler, Julie and Claudia Schwabe. "Fairy Tales and Folktales." Last modified February 22, 2018. Accessed March 21, 2020. https://www.oxfordbibliographies.com/view/document/obo-9780199791231/obo-9780199791231-0195.xml.

Kynes, Sandra. *Llewellyn's Complete Book of Correspondences: A Comprehensive & Cross-Referenced Resource for Pagans & Wiccans.* Woodbury: Llewellyn Publications, 2013.

Lagay, Faith, PhD. "The Legacy of Humoral Medicine." *AMA Journal of Ethics: Illuminating the Art of Medicine.* Published July 2002. Accessed December 7, 2019. https://journalofethics.ama-assn.org/article/legacy-humoral-medicine/2002-07

Leonora, Inga. "Quarters, Elements, & the Problem of Direction." Australis Incognita—Old Craft in Australia. Posted September 1, 2014, accessed December 7, 2019.https://australisincognita.wordpress.com/2014/09/01/quarters-elements-the-problem-of-direction/

Lévi, Éliphas. *The Paradoxes of the Highest Science.* Second ed. Translator unknown. Pomeroy: Health Research Books, 1996.

Lewis, James R. *Witchcraft Today: An Encyclopedia of Wiccan and Neopagan Traditions.* Santa Barbara: ABC-CLIO Inc., 1999.

Livingstone, David. *The Dying God: The Hidden History of Western Civilization.* Bloomington: IUniverse, 2002.

MacLir, Algerian Gwydion. *The Witch's Wand: The Craft, Lore, and Magick of Wands and Staffs.* Woodbury: Llewellyn Publications, 2015.

Malamut, Melissa. "Witch Population Doubles as Millennials Cast Off Christianity." *New York Post.* Published November 20, 2018, accessed December 28, 2019. https://nypost.com/2018/11/20/witch-population-doubles-as-millennials-cast-off-christianity/.

Mankey, Jason. *Transformative Witchcraft: The Greater Mysteries.* Woodbury: Llewellyn Publications, 2019.

Mankey, Jason. *The Witch's Wheel of the Year: Rituals for Circles, Solitaries, and Covens.* Woodbury: Llewellyn Publications, 2019.

Melville, Francis. *The Book of Faeries: A Guide to the World of Elves, Pixies, Goblins, and Other Magic Spirits.* Hong Kong: Regent Publishing Services Ltd., 2002.

Sthorpe11. "Mercuralia—Festival of Mercury." *Creating History.* Published May 14, 2013. Accessed May 1, 2020. http://www.creatinghistory.com/mercuralia-festival-of-mercury/

Meredith, Jane, and Gede Parma. *Elements of Magic: Reclaiming Earth Air, Fire, Water, and Spirit.* Woodbury, Llewellyn Publications, 2018.

Morita, Kiyoko. *The Book of Incense: Enjoying the Traditional Art of Japanese Scents.* Tokyo: Kodansha International, 2006.

Mynott, Jeremy. *Birds in the Ancient World: Winged Wonders.* Oxford: Oxford University Press, 2018.

Napoli, Donna Jo. *Treasury of Norse Mythology: Stories of Intrigue, Trickery, Love, and Revenge.* Washington DC: National Geographic, 2015.

Nigg, Joseph. *The Book of Dragons and Other Mythical Beasts.* New York: Quarto, 2002.

Nigg, Joseph. *The Book of Fabulous Beasts: A Treasury of Writings from Ancient Times to the Present.* New York: Oxford University Press, 1999.

Online Etymology Dictionary. "Daimon." Accessed 12.28.19. https://www.etymonline.com/word/daimon.

Online Etymology Dictionary. "Demon." Accessed 12.28.19. https://www.etymonline.com/word/demon.

Page, Sophie. "Medieval Magic." In *The Oxford Illustrated History of Witchcraft & Magic*, edited by Owen Davies, 29-64. Oxford: Oxford University Press, 2017.

Parma, Gede. *Spirited: Taking Paganism Beyond the Circle.* Woodbury: Llewellyn Publications, 2009.

Perrone, Bobette, H. Henrietta Stockel, and Victoria Krueger. *Medicine Women, Curanderas, and Women Doctors.* Norman: University of Oklahoma Press, 1989.

Peoples, Hervey C., Pavel Duda, and Frank W. Marlowe. "Hunter-Gatherers and the Origins of Religion." *Human Nature (Hawthorne, N.Y.)* vol. 27,3 (2016): 261-82.

Phillips, Barty. *The Book of Herbs: An Illustrated A-Z of the World's Most Popular Culinary and Medicinal Plants.* Springville: Hobble Creek Press, 2006.

Pollio, Marcus Vitruvius, trans. by Joseph Gwilt. *The Architecture of M. Vitruvius Pollio in Ten Books.* London: The British Library, 1823.

Quinlan, Ginger. *Scents of the Soul: Creating Herbal Incense for Body, Mind, and Spirit.* Forres: Findhorn Press, 2009.

Rankine, David, and Sorita D'Este. *Practical Elemental Magick: A Guide to the Four Elements (Air, Fire, Water, and Earth) in the Western Esoteric Tradition.* Glastonbury: Avalonia, 2008.

Renfrew, Colin. *Prehistory: The Making of the Human Mind.* New York: Modern Library, 2008.

Rogo, D. Scott. *Leaving the Body: A Complete Guide to Astral Projection.* New York: Fireside, 1983.

Roth, Harold. *The Witching Herbs: 13 Essential Plants and Herbs for Your Magical Garden.* Newburyport: Red Wheel, 2017.

Russell, Jeffrey Burton. *Witchcraft in the Middle Ages.* Ithaca: Cornell University Press, 1972.

Schalen, Leonard. *The Alphabet Versus the Goddess: The Conflict Between Word and Image.* London: Penguin, 1999.

Schumann, Walter. *Gemstones of the World.* Fifth Edition, revised. Sterling: New York, 2013.

Shuker, Dr. Karl. *Dragons: A Natural History.* New York: Simon and Schuster, 1995.

Siculus, Diodorus. *Library of History, Book IV.* University of Chicago. Accessed September 9, 2019.http://penelope.uchicago .edu/Thayer/E/Roman/Texts/Diodorus_Siculus/4C*.html.

Smith, Ryan. *The Way of Fire and Ice: The Living Tradition of Norse Paganism.* Woodbury: Llewellyn Publications, 2019.

Smith, Steven R. *Wylundt's Book of Incense.* Newburyport: Weiser Books, 1996.

Spencer, Ezzie. *Lunar Abundance: Cultivating Joy, Peace, and Purpose Using the Phases of the Moon.* Philadelphia: Running Press Adult, 2018.

Sperlin, Ottis Bedney. *Studies in English-World Literature.* New York: Century Company, 1923.

Stone, Merlin. *When God Was A Woman.* New York: Harcourt Brace & Company, 1976.

Toll, Maia. *The Illustrated Herbiary: Guidance and Rituals from 36 Bewitching Botanicals.* North Adams: Storey Publishing, 2018.

Voltmer, Rita. "The Witch Trials." In *The Oxford Illustrated History of Witchcraft & Magic*, edited by Owen Davies, 97-133. Oxford: Oxford University Press, 2017.

Webster, Richard. *Llewellyn's Complete Book of Divination: Your Definitive Source for Learning Predictive and Prophetic Techniques.* Woodbury: Llewellyn Publications, 2017.

Weigle, Martha. *Spiders & Spinsters: Women and Mythology.* Albuquerque: University of New Mexico Press, 1982.

White, T.H. *The Book of Beasts: Being a Translation from a Latin Bestiary of the Twelfth Century.* New York: Dover Publications, 1984.

Whitehurst, Tess. *The Magic of Flowers: A Guide to their Metaphysical Uses and Properties.* Woodbury: Llewellyn Publications, 2013.

Wilkinson, Toby. *The Rise and Fall of Ancient Egypt.* London: A&C Black, 2011.

Williamson, Cecil. "468—Print." Museum of Witchcraft and Magic. Accessed September 9, 2019. https://museumofwitchcraftandmagic.co.uk/object/print-5/.

Willoughby, Jean. *Nature's Remedies: An Illustrated Guide to Healing Herbs.* San Francisco: Chronicle Books LLC, 2016.

Zagami, Leo Lyon. *The Invisible Master: Secret Chiefs, Unknown Superiors, and the Puppet Masters Who Pull the Strings of Occult Power from the Alien World.* San Francisco: CCC Publishing, 2018.

Zakroff, Laura Tempest. *Sigil Witchery: A Guide To Crafting Magick Symbols.* Woodbury: Llewellyn Publications, 2018.

INDEX

INDEX